DK EYEWITNESS

TOP
DUBROVNIK
AND THE DALMATIAN COAST

Top 10 Dubrovnik and the Dalmatian Coast Highlights

The Top 10 of Everything

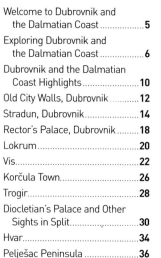

CONTENTS

Dubrovnik and the Dalmatian Coast Area by Area

Streetsmart

Within each Top 10 list in this book, no hierarchy of quality or popularity is implied. All 10 are, in the editor's opinion, of roughly equal merit.

Title page, front cover and spine Cathedral of the Assumption of the Virgin Mary, Old Town *Back cover, clockwise from top left* Vis Island; Interior of St. Domnius Cathedral; Sunset over Dubrovnik; Old Town; Street in Old Town

The information in this DK Eyewitness Top 10 Travel Guide is checked regularly. Every effort has been made to ensure that this book is as up-to-date as possible at the time of going to press. Some details, however, such as telephone numbers, opening hours, prices, gallery hanging arrangements and travel information, are liable to change. The publishers cannot accept responsibility for any consequences arising from the use of this book, nor for any material on third-party websites, and cannot guarantee that any website address in this book will be a suitable source of travel information. We value the views and suggestions of our readers very highly. Please write to: Publisher, DK Eyewitness Travel Guides, Dorling Kindersley, 80 Strand, London WC2R 0RL, Great Britain, or email travelguides@dk.com

Welcome to
Dubrovnik and the Dalmatian Coast

An ancient walled town jutting seaward from a mountainous coast, Dubrovnik is one of the Mediterranean's most beguiling destinations. It stands on a dramatic stretch of coastline, with historic ports wedged into its bays and inlets, and a clutch of idyllic islands just a short ferry ride offshore. With Eyewitness Top 10 Dubrovnik and the Dalmatian Coast, it is yours to explore.

Despite its compact size, Dubrovnik's Old City is packed with fine sights, such as the ornate **Rector's Palace**, and the **Franciscan Monastery**, the **Stradun** and evocative backstreets lined with Renaissance town houses. With some of Croatia's best bars and restaurants squeezed into its narrow alleys, this is one medieval city with a decidedly contemporary edge.

Northwest of Dubrovnik, the bustling port of **Split** started out as the retirement home of Roman emperor Diocletian, whose palace still forms the city's vibrant core. Ferries run from Split to the Dalmatian islands of **Hvar**, **Korčula** and **Vis**, where chic nightspots and swanky yachting marinas rub shoulders with olive groves, wild nature and a stunning variety of beaches. Wherever you go, you will find delightfully clear seas – perfect for swimming, snorkelling or kayaking.

Whether you're visiting for a weekend, a week, or longer, our Top 10 guide brings together the best of everything the region has to offer, from Dubrovnik's city walls to the most secluded island beaches. The guide has useful tips throughout, from seeking out what's free to splashing out on the best Dalmatian wines, plus six easy-to-follow itineraries designed to tie together a clutch of sights in a short space of time. Add inspiring photography and detailed maps, and you've got the essential pocket-sized travel companion. **Enjoy the book, and enjoy Dubrovnik and the Dalmatian Coast.**

Clockwise from top: **Bay near Hvar town, lion sculpture in a portal at Trogir's Cathedral of St Lawrence, the Old Harbour in Dubrovnik, Orebić town, Dubrovnik lace, Neretva Delta, a pavement café in Dubrovnik**

Exploring Dubrovnik and the Dalmatian Coast

The area surrounding Dubrovnik boasts historic cities, wild landscapes and crystal-clear seas. To make the most of your stay and help you to get a flavour of this fascinating region, here are some ideas for two-day and seven-day Dalmatian jaunts.

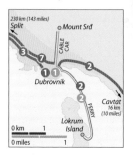

Dubrovnik's 14th-century **Franciscan Monastery** dominates the western end of the city.

Two Days in Dubrovnik

Day ❶
MORNING
Begin with a circuit of **Dubrovnik's city walls** (see pp12–13) to take in some fabulous views of the Old City. Continue with a stroll down the **Stradun** (see pp14–15), Dubrovnik's set-piece main street.
AFTERNOON
Relive the glory of the Dubrovnik Republic with a visit to the **Rector's Palace** (see pp18–19). Next, soak up the historic atmosphere of Dubrovnik by wandering through the **Pustijerna quarter** (see p70).

Day ❷
MORNING
Admire Renaissance artworks at the **Franciscan Monastery** (see pp16–17)

before taking the cable car to **Mount Srđ** (see p71) to see the stunning panorama of the coast.
AFTERNOON
Take a boat to the island of **Lokrum** (see pp20–21), a self-contained world of semi-wild gardens and stunning coastal paths. On your return, admire the sculptures in the **Museum of Modern Art** (see p67).

Seven Days in Dalmatia

Day ❶
Follow day 1 of the two-day Dubrovnik itinerary.

Day ❷
Spend the morning exploring **Lokrum** (see pp20–21), a beautiful island of lush greenery and rocky bays. Afterwards, head south to

Set around the Cathedral of St Stephen, the main square in Hvar town is lined with impressive Renaissance buildings.

Key
— Two-day itinerary
— Seven-day itinerary

Cavtat *(see p96)* for a late lunch on the palm-shaded waterfront. Return to Dubrovnik via Sokol grad *(see p97)* for a taste of stark inland scenery.

Day ❸
Travel from Dubrovnik to Split, pausing to enjoy the long pebble beaches of the **Makarska Riviera** *(see pp86–93)*. Spend a couple of hours exploring the medieval town of **Trogir** *(see pp28–9)* before ending the day in Split. Spend the evening strolling the bustling **Diocletian's Palace** quarter *(see pp30–31)*.

Day ❹
Leave Split by ferry for the laid-back island of **Vis** *(see pp22–3)*. Stroll around Vis town before crossing the island to the historic fishing port of Komiža. In the afternoon, take a fast boat from Komiža harbour to the islet of **Biševo** *(see p81)* and its Blue Cave. Return to Komiža for a sumptuous seafood dinner.

Day ❺
If it's a Tuesday, travel direct by catamaran from Vis town to **Hvar town** *(see p34)*. Otherwise, return to Split and take the car ferry to Hvar island's main port, Stari Grad. Hire a vehicle to tour the island *(see pp34–5)*, taking in the pretty fishing port of **Jelsa**, as well as the Renaissance splendours of Hvar town. The town's chic bars and trendy clubs may well keep you occupied until morning.

Day ❻
Providing you book in advance, the morning catamaran from Hvar town will get you to **Korčula town** *(see pp26–7)* early enough to take a pre-lunch amble through this historic peninsula settlement. Grab a bite at **Adio Mare** *(see p83)* before heading to the sandy beaches of **Lumbarda** *(see p49)*, just outside Korčula town, for a spot of swimming and sunbathing.

Day ❼
Take the ferry from Korčula to Orebić and drive along the **Pelješac Peninsula** *(see pp36–7)*, stopping for lunch at the gourmet town of Ston. Afterwards, continue to Dubrovnik, arriving in time for an evening cable-car trip up **Mount Srđ** *(see p71)*.

Some of the region's best beaches are in Orebić, on the Pelješac Peninsula.

Top 10 Dubrovnik and the Dalmatian Coast Highlights

Aerial view of Dubrovnik's historic town and the island of Lokrum

TOP 10 Dubrovnik and the Dalmatian Coast Highlights

The Dalmatian coast is one of Europe's most stunning escapes. Long stretches of glorious shoreline are framed between limestone mountains and the Adriatic, where hundreds of islands await exploration. The coastline is punctuated by a series of lively towns and cities, in which the region's long and eclectic history comes alive in wonderfully preserved "old cores".

1 Old City Walls, Dubrovnik

For centuries, these remarkable city walls have afforded Dubrovnik protection. Today they allow visitors a bird's-eye view of this impressive city *(see pp12–13)*.

2 Stradun, Dubrovnik

Along its polished expanse, Dubrovnik's pedestrianized main thoroughfare boasts churches, palaces, shops, fountains and pavement cafés *(see pp14–17)*.

3 Rector's Palace, Dubrovnik

Under the Republic of Ragusa, the city's figurehead presided here, amid Gothic and Renaissance architecture. This impressive palace has been reinvented as a museum and cultural venue *(see pp18–19)*.

4 Lokrum

Mediterranean gardens combine with rocky beaches and untrammelled nature to make this small island an essential trip from Dubrovnik, just to the north *(see pp20–21)*.

5 Vis

This compact island is bursting with history and natural beauty, with the central massif of Mount Hum book-ended by the charming ports of Komiža and Vis town. With the widest range of seafood in the Adriatic, it's also a foodie haven *(see pp22–3)*.

6 Korčula Town

It is not, as some claim, the birthplace of Marco Polo, but Korčula town is simply sublime, set on its own peninsula. Its cathedral is one of the most charming ecclesiastical buildings in the Adriatic *(see pp26–7)*.

7 Trogir

Set on its own island, this perfectly preserved old city dazzles with churches, palaces and one of Europe's most striking cathedrals, whose beauty is recognized by UNESCO *(see pp28–9)*.

8 Diocletian's Palace, Split

The palatial, UNESCO World Heritage-listed retirement home of Emperor Diocletian forms the frenetic heart of the dashing Mediterranean city of Split *(see pp30–33)*.

BOSNIA & HERZEGOVINA

Vrgorac
Gradac
Metković
Ploče
Opuzen

10 Pelješac Peninsula
Ston • Mali Ston

Mljet

1 2 3 Dubrovnik
4 Cavtat
Lokrum

0 km 25
0 miles 25

Herceg-Novi •

9 Hvar

Of all Croatia's islands, Hvar arguably offers most variety. Swanky marinas sit alongside fashionable destinations, family resorts, ancient villages and secluded beaches *(see pp34–5)*.

10 Pelješac Peninsula

A mountainous finger of land poking west from the Dalmatian coast, Pelješac is ideal for beach-combers and offers great wines and seafood *(see pp36–7)*.

TOP 10 ⭐ Old City Walls, Dubrovnik

Dubrovnik's city walls, up to 6 m (20 ft) thick and 22 m (72 ft) high, are a stunning sight. A cradle of stone, they helped protect one of Europe's most perfectly preserved medieval cities, as well as safeguarding the independence of the city-state for centuries. Running from the steep cliffs in the north to the Adriatic in the south, they proved impenetrable to pirates and potential conquerors until the keys were handed to the French on 31 January 1808, and the Republic of Dubrovnik (or Ragusa, its former name) ended.

3 Ploče Gate
The bridge leading to the Ploče Gate, on the eastern walls, offers new arrivals tantalizing glimpses of the city and the old port.

4 Revelin Fort
Near the eastern walls, this 16th-century fortress is used for exhibitions, plus music and dancing in summer.

Aerial view of Old City

1 Pile Gate
This entrance (above) to the Old City leads, via a drawbridge, down on to the Stradun. Look out for the figure of Dubrovnik's patron saint, St Blaise, above the gate and, a little further on, a more modern depiction of him by Ivan Meštrović.

2 Minčeta Fort
North of the Pile Gate, steep steps lead up to an impressive fort (below). Views at sunset from this 15th-century bastion justify the exertion to reach it.

5 Bokar Fort
This Renaissance fort (above), designed by Michelozzo Michelozzi, watches over the city's original port. From here, the Lovrijenac Fortress is visible across the water.

6 St Luke's Fortress
Overlooking the port, this 13th-century fortification is a semicircular bastion where sea-facing cannons were housed. Part of the fortress is now occupied by a restaurant and bar.

LIBERTAS

Dubrovnik's daunting city walls are just part of the reason why the Republic of Ragusa enjoyed centuries of independence, at a time when the Venetians and Ottomans were vying for territory all around the Adriatic. Machiavelli would have applauded the skill of the republic's negotiators as they played off the various powers against each other, dipping into the city's bountiful gold reserves when all else failed. The word proudly flown on their flag was *Libertas* (freedom).

Map of the Old City Walls

❷ ❶ ❺ ❹ ❸ ❻ ❽ ❾ ❼

PELINE
OD PUSTIJERNE
PRIJEKO
PLACA (STRADUN)
OD PUČA
LUŽA
GUNDULIĆEVA POLJANA
OD KAŠTELA
ISPOD MIRA

⑩ Rooftops

The legacy of the 1991–2 siege is evident from the stretch of wall around the old port. From here the contrast between the charming, original roof tiles and the newer replacements, imported from France and Slovenia, is very easy to see.

⑦ Maritime Museum

Part of St John's Fortress is a museum *(see pp46–7)* that sheds light on the Republic of Ragusa's rich and eclectic maritime heritage. The exhibits include a large collection of model ships, sepia photographs of the port and historic maps.

⑧ Boat Trip

For a completely different perspective of Dubrovnik's walls, join a tour boat or hire a local water taxi (both leave from the old port) and skirt around the base of the city **(below)**, where the Adriatic swishes against the rocks and the ramparts soar menacingly upward.

⑨ St John's Fort

This fortification protected the old port from advancing enemy ships and was, in its time, at the cutting edge of military technology. Begun in the 1300s, it was added to well into the 16th century.

NEED TO KNOW

MAP E9 ▪ Access the walls from the Stradun (next to the Pile Gate), by St John's Fort and St Luke's Fortress

Open Apr–May, Aug–Sep: 8am–6:30pm daily; Jun–Jul: 8am–7:30pm; Oct: 8am–5:30pm; Nov–Mar: 9am–3pm

Adm 150kn; children 50kn; audio guide available

Maritime Museum: **MAP H10**; 020 323 904; open Apr–Oct: 9am–6pm daily; Nov–Mar: 9am–4pm Tue–Sun; adm 120kn (incl entry to other sites); children/students 25kn

▪ Buža *(see p74)*, outside the southern walls, is a bar worth seeking out for drinks and great views. From the Jesuit Church, follow the "cold drinks" sign.

▪ The walls can be very crowded in summer, so arrive early to avoid the queues. Carry water, as refreshment opportunities are limited.

🔟⭐ **Stradun, Dubrovnik**

The sweeping Stradun, also known as the Placa, is Dubrovnik's main thoroughfare, cutting a pedestrianized swathe through the Old City. It was formed when the narrow channel that separated the Slavic settlement of Dubrovnik on the mainland from the Roman settlement on the island of Raus was filled in during the 12th century. Today this limestone walkway, with its shops, cafés and restaurants, buzzes with visitors.

THE EARTHQUAKE OF 1667

This earthquake tore the heart out of Gothic and Renaissance Dubrovnik, killing 2,500 citizens and destroying many key buildings. This terrible tragedy led to the construction of one of the most impressive Baroque cities in Europe. Carefully planned to sit within the protective confines of the sturdy city walls, it resisted all intruders until the arrival of Napoleonic troops in the early 19th century.

1 Sponza Palace
The inscription "We are forbidden to cheat and use false measures, and when I weigh goods, God weighs me" reveals this early 16th-century palace's former role as customs house and mint **(above)**. Today it is home to the State Archives.

2 Café Culture
Join the locals for a drink and watch the world go by. Many cafés set tables out at the first glimpse of sunshine, but getting a seat can be an ordeal at the height of summer.

4 Shutters and Lamps
For a controlled piece of town planning, look at the window shutters and the lamps along the Stradun. They are all the same shade of green, giving a cohesion rare in European cities today.

The bustling Stradun

3 Onofrio's Large Fountain
Damaged in the siege of 1991–2, this 15th-century fountain **(below)** has been restored. It is named after the architect of the city's water-supply system.

5 Orlando's Column
Mystery surrounds the statue that guards the spot where the Stradun unfurls into Luža Square. Some locals claim that Orlando was a legendary knight who saved the city from disaster when he fought off menacing pirates in the 8th century.

6 Onofrio's Little Fountain

Tucked into a building by the Rector's Palace, this "little sister" to Onofrio's Large Fountain often goes unnoticed. It dates from the 15th century.

Plan of the Stradun

9 Clocktower

This striking timepiece **(left)** dates from the 15th century. Overhauled in 1929, the duo of bell strikers visible today are copies. The originals are housed in the city's Sponza Palace.

7 Church of St Saviour

The staid Renaissance façade does little to hint at the colour inside. Here regular concerts and art exhibitions are held, often with work by modern Dalmatian artists.

10 Church of St Blaise

This church **(below)** sits at the top of the Stradun. Inside, Dubrovnik's patron saint, St Blaise, cradles a model of the city showing what it looked like before the earthquake of 1667.

8 Franciscan Monastery

The dark cloisters and lush vegetation of this 14th-century monastery *(see p16)* conjure up echoes of the Dubrovnik of old, as do the fascinating exhibits of the Monastery Museum *(see p17)*. Make sure you arrive early to avoid the crowds.

NEED TO KNOW

Church of St Saviour: **MAP F8**; open 9am–4pm daily

Franciscan Monastery and Museum: **MAP F8**; open Apr–Oct: 9am–6pm daily; Nov–Mar: 9am–2pm (to 5pm for groups by appt); closed 25 Dec; adm 40kn; children 20kn

Church of St Blaise: **MAP G9**; open 8am–8pm daily

Memorial Room of the Dubrovnik Defenders: **MAP G9**; Sponza Palace; 020 321 032; open May–Oct: 9am–9pm daily; Nov–Apr: 10am–3pm

■ The Café Festival, housed in a graceful stone house, is the place to be and be seen on the Stradun. During the Dubrovnik Summer Festival, you will have to be quick to snare one of the coveted outside tables.

■ Even if you have seen the Stradun by day, you should also return at night, when floodlighting gives the thoroughfare a more romantic ambience.

Franciscan Monastery, Stradun

The inner courtyard of the monastery

1 Inner Courtyard

Step into this inner sanctum to view the cloisters and admire the spectacular balustrade that frames the courtyard.

2 Romanesque Cloisters

Mihoje Brajkov's magnificent 14th-century cloisters, with their graceful double-pillared columns, deserve a close look. These can be visited between 9am and 6pm.

3 Frescoes

The life of St Francis and his animals is depicted in the frescoes that line the cloisters.

4 Bell Tower

The dome-topped bell tower dominating the western end of the Stradun dates

from the 14th century and features Gothic and Romanesque elements. Its majestic presence towers over the monastery courtyard.

5 Pharmacy

The monastery is home to one of the oldest pharmacies in Europe, with a collection of treatments and pharmacopoeias dating from the 15th century. The dispensary is still operational (7am–7pm Mon–Sat).

6 Church of St Francis

Most of the original 14th-century church was destroyed by the 1667 earthquake. Remarkable features in this 17th-century reconstruction include the lavish marble altars and the ornate organ framed by cherubs.

7 Library

The monastery is home to Croatia's largest collection of historical manuscripts, over 3,000, dating from the early Middle Ages.

8 Portraits

The library walls are adorned with portraits of some of the city's most celebrated citizens, including Marin Getaldić, a 17th-century mathematician and physicist.

9 Ivan Gundulić Memorial

A plaque on the north wall of the church commemorates the poet Ivan Gundulić (1589–1638), who is buried in the church.

10 Gothic Portal

A *Pietà* by brothers Petar and Leonardo Petrović crowns the southern portal, all that remains of the original 14th-century church.

Pietà **by the Petrović brothers**

Franciscan Monastery Museum

1 Dubrovnik Painting
The background of Nikola Božidarević's *Madonna and Child* painting shows how medieval Dubrovnik looked before the devastating earthquake of 1667.

2 Missile Damage
On 6 December 1991, known locally as "Black Tuesday", Serbian missiles rained down on Dubrovnik. Two shell-holes have been left in the museum walls to serve as reminders of the damage sustained by the monastery.

Stone relief of St Francis

3 War Record
Inconspicuously located below the painting of Dubrovnik is a book cataloguing the devastation caused by the 54 direct hits upon the monastery during the siege of the city in 1991–2.

4 Missiles
Tucked into a corner, by a bench near the entrance to the museum, lie the casings of some of the missiles that wrought destruction on this tranquil space.

5 St Blaise's Foot
The most prized possession in the reliquary collection is this foot of St Blaise, preserved in a boot-like gold-and-silver case.

6 Osman
One of the treasures of the monastery's library is an 18th-century transcript of Ivan Gundulić's *Osman*. Heralded as the poet's masterpiece, it celebrates a famous Slavic victory over the Turks.

7 Potions and Poisons
Set in a recreation of the monastery's original pharmacy are row upon row of measuring instruments, traditional remedies and some lethal poisons.

8 St Francis
The medieval stone relief of St Francis, above the museum entrance, appears to be casting a protective eye over his domain.

9 Stone Reliefs
A small open space to one side of the museum contains odd remnants of carved masonry from the building, including gargoyles and segments of old gravestones.

10 Religious Exhibits
The museum houses several 15th- and 16th-century icons, a crucifix by Blaž Jurjev Trogiranin dating from 1428, as well as a beautiful 15th-century polyptych by Lovro Marinov Dobričević, which features a portrait of St Blaise.

A 16th-century icon depicting the Annunciation

🔟 ⭐ Rector's Palace, Dubrovnik

Nominal head of the government, the Rector of Dubrovnik was in office for one month and was only allowed to leave the palace on official business. The original medieval castle that stood here, was blown up in 1435. The Gothic-Renaissance palace built in its place had to be restored after another explosion in 1463 and again after the 1667 earthquake. Dubrovnik no longer has a rector. His opulent residence now houses the Cultural History Museum.

Gothic Portico ③
The ornately carved portico **(right)** was built using stone from the Dalmatian island of Korčula. In the middle of the parade of Gothic columns and capitals are three in the Renaissance style.

① Stairs
The rather ghoulish stairs **(above)** up to the first floor are adorned with three lifelike hands on each rail. They were used only on ceremonial occasions, when the Rector received visitors.

④ Gundulić Portrait
This is one of the few portraits in existence of Dubrovnik's most celebrated poet, Ivan Gundulić (1589–1638).

Statue of Miho Pracat ②
Taking pride of place in the atrium is Pietro Giacometti's 17th-century statue of shipping magnate Miho Pracat **(right)**, from the nearby island of Lopud. Dying without an heir, Pracat left his wealth to the Republic of Ragusa.

⑤ Atrium
A compact open-air space **(left)** that offers a suitably grand welcome to visitors, the historical atrium also serves as a unique venue for many cultural events, such as recitals by the Dubrovnik Symphony Orchestra.

AN EXPLOSIVE HISTORY

In addition to being the abode of the head of the Republic of Ragusa, as well as the site of the law courts and prison, the Rector's Palace also once served as a gunpowder store. This foolishness on the part of the authorities unfortunately resulted in several explosions that caused damage to the building. It was only after a second disastrous explosion that the city's leaders finally made the decision to move the gunpowder elsewhere.

⑥ Statues of St Blaise

The sculptures of St Blaise in the museum here afford visitors a rare opportunity to get up close to the city's patron saint. Most other renderings hang well above head height, or behind distant glass in his eponymous church *(see p45)*.

Key
■ First floor
■ Ground floor

Plan of the Rector's Palace

⑦ Prison Cells

The ground floor once served as the Republic of Ragusa's courtroom and prison. The dank, gloomy cells hint at the harsh treatment of inmates, who relied on friends and family for food and water.

⑧ Inscription

The notice in Latin at the top of the stairs would have put the Grand Council members in their place by reminding them of their duty to focus, not on personal concerns, but only on public and civic matters.

⑨ Sedan Chairs

A collection of 18th-century sedan chairs **(right)**, is found on the first floor and at other locations in the palace. These chairs offer a hint of the opulence of the city's nobility.

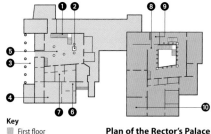

⑩ Rector's Study

In the study, one of the most elegant and graceful rooms in the palace, visitors are able to admire the 16th-century painting *The Baptism of Christ* by Mihajlo Hamzić (1460–1518) and a cabinet painted by Luca Giordano (1634–1705).

NEED TO KNOW

MAP G9 ■ Pred Dvorom 3
■ 020 321 422

Open Apr–Oct: 9am–6pm daily; Nov–Mar: 9am–4pm daily; closed 1 Jan, 3 Feb, 25 Dec

Adm 120kn (incl entry to other sites); groups 100 kn; children 25kn

■ The Gradska Kavana *(see p74)* is a café fit for a rector, with stunning views across the Luža Square and down the Stradun on one side and out on to the historic old port on the other.

■ The windows on the first floor make a perfect spot for photographing both the cathedral and the displays of folk dancing that sometimes take place in the street below.

TOP 10 ⭐ Lokrum

A short distance offshore, the lush green island of Lokrum is a real contrast to the bustle of Dubrovnik. A UNESCO-protected reserve, the island is covered with indigenous and tropical vegetation, while its coast offers some of Dubrovnik's best sunbathing and swimming. The former Benedictine monastery, turned into a holiday home by Austrian Archduke Maximilian and later used as a set for the TV show *Game of Thrones*, provides a strong historical focus.

The Boat Landing ①

Exploration of the island begins at the boat landing **(right)**, over-looked by the so-called Hunter's Lodge. A peach-coloured villa built in Archduke Maximilian's time, the lodge is now a park information centre and exhibition space.

② The "Dead Sea" Lake

One of Lokrum's most popular bathing areas is this unusually buoyant saltwater lake **(below)** just inland from the island's southeastern tip.

③ Benedictine Monastery

Founded in the 15th century, Lokrum's Benedictine Monastery was a major seat of learning until its dissolution in 1798. Archduke Maximilian bought it in 1859 but preserved many of its features – notably the elegant cloisters, where you will now find a restaurant and café.

④ Visitor Centre

The visitor centre, in a wing of the monastery, is largely devoted to the TV show *Game of Thrones*, scenes of which were shot in the cloisters. There is an interactive map of locations seen in the series and a selection of stage props, including the iron throne used by the rulers of King's Landing.

NEED TO KNOW

MAP H6

■ www.lokrum.hr

Passenger boats run from the Old City's harbour every hour (every half-hour in peak season) from April to November, taking less than 15 minutes.

A return ticket (150kn adults, 25kn children) covers all of the island's attractions, which remain open from the arrival of the first boat (10am, depending on season) to the departure of the last (6pm).

·······

■ Just up from the boat landing and enclosed by well-trimmed hedges is a pleasant open-air café, frequented by the island's free-roaming peacocks.

■ It is forbidden to pick plants or to stay on the island overnight.

■ There is a restaurant in the former monastery building, but Lokrum is a great place for a picnic. Choose a bench beside the Educational Path, or spread your blanket on the olive-shade lawns beside the monastery.

7 The Monastery Gardens

South of the monastery buildings are terraces featuring geometrically laid-out box hedges **(left)** and rose gardens. They were planted by Archduke Maximilian, who planned to turn the whole island into a park.

GAME OF THRONES

The famous cast and crew of the fantasy TV series *Game of Thrones*, will return to Dubrovnik to film the final season (2018–19). The city itself doubled as the fictional capital city King's Landing before, with many of Dubrovnik's trademark features (such as the medieval walls and Lovrijenac Fortress) becoming an integral part of the show's visual style. Other locations included Lokrum's monastery cloisters, which were used for a garden-party scene in Qarth, and Klis Fortress near Split *(see p88)*, which was the ideal setting for the hilltop city of Meereen.

5 Botanical Gardens

A striking collection of plants from Australia, Africa and South America fill this large enclosure, established in 1959 by the National Academy of Science and Art. The garden, part of the Institute for Marine and Coastal Research, features over 70 kinds of eucalyptus and towering cacti.

8 Educational Path

Leading north from the botanical gardens is this well-maintained coastal path. Dating from Archduke Maximilian's time, it makes an almost complete circuit of the island. Signboards alert visitors to the local flora, which includes groves of holm oak and South European ash.

Map of Lokrum Island

6 Fort Royal

Located on the summit of 97-m (318-ft) Glavica Hill, Lokrum's highest point, this circular fortress **(below)** was built by the French in 1806, straight after their takeover of the Adriatic coast. It overlooks a forest of Aleppo pine trees imported by the Austrians in the 19th century.

9 Naturist Beach

The terraced rock formations east of the monastery gardens feature plenty of stony platforms ideal for sunbathing. A cult spot among nudists for decades, the eastern shore is now an officially designated naturist beach.

10 Ruined Basilica

Just outside the monastery are the impressive remains of a three-aisled Romanesque basilica. Dating from the 12th century, it attests to the importance of Lokrum in the religious life of the Republic of Ragusa.

TOP 10 ⭐ Vis

Compact, mountainous and full of history, Vis is one of the Adriatic's most compelling island destinations. Further from the mainland than Croatia's other major islands, it has long held strategic importance for those wishing to control the Adriatic. Vis opened up to tourism in the early 1990s while it was still serving as a major Yugoslav army base, and it still retains an unspoiled, non-commercialized feel. Thanks to its rich fisheries, Vis is a fabulous place to sample traditional Adriatic seafood.

1 Vis Town

Stretching along the shores of a broad bay, the island's main settlement boasts a wealth of ancient Greek, Roman and Renaissance remains. The seafront is packed with yachts in the summer **(right)**, and there are some wonderful restaurants serving local specialities.

2 Mount Hum

At 587 m (1,926 ft) above sea level, Vis's highest point offers stunning Adriatic views, with the port of Komiža below and the islands of Biševo, Jabuka and Svetac to the west. On a clear day, you can see all the way to Italy's coast.

3 Komiža

Curled round a steep-sided bay **(above)**, the former capital of the Adriatic anchovy-fishing industry is today a charming port.

4 King George III Fortress

Built by the British in 1813, and currently serving as a bar, restaurant and nightclub, this sturdy hilltop fortress contains a small museum devoted to the island's military history and offers sweeping views from its tower.

5 Kut

Squeezed into a corner of the bay, this quiet suburb of Vis town was where the 16th-century nobles of Hvar built their summer houses. Still filled with elegant stone villas overlooking narrow streets, it preserves an aristocratic air.

6 Submarine Pens

Built to house the Yugoslav navy's pocket submarines, these concrete tunnels **(below)** outside Vis town are popular with nautical tourists, who can sail small craft inside. They are also accessible on foot or by bike.

7 Tito's Cave

Vis served as the headquarters of Yugoslavia's Partisan movement in 1944, when Marshal Tito presided over top-level meetings in this cave on the side of Mount Hum. It is now bare, with the exception of a few inscriptions, but it is still a popular site of political pilgrimage.

Map of Vis

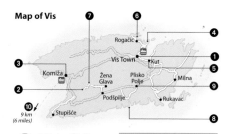

9 Plisko Polje

This village sits on the edge of a lush green plain that produces most of the island's fruit, vegetables and wine – particularly Vugava, the dry white wine that is indigenous to Vis.

10 The Blue Cave

Excursion boats and motor dinghies speed across the water from Komiža to the island of Biševo, where the unique Blue Cave is one of Croatia's most visited natural wonders, illuminated by refracted turquoise light.

Stiniva 8

One of the Adriatic's most celebrated coves **(right)**, Stiniva boasts a small shingle beach enclosed by curving rocky promontories. Some distance from the road, it can only be reached on foot or by mountain bike.

WARTIME VIS

During World War II, Dalmatia was occupied by Italian forces. The Adriatic coast was liberated by Yugoslav Partisans, led by Josip Broz Tito, and reunited with the rest of Croatia. From June to September 1944, the headquarters of Tito's Partisan movement was on Vis, which became heavily garrisoned and protected by Britain and the US. The British built an airfield on the south of the island, while Tito held meetings in a cave.

NEED TO KNOW

MAP B5 ■ Tourist Office: Šetalište Stare Isse, Vis town; 021 717 017; www.tz-vis.hr ■ Travel agencies include Alternatura (Komiža; 021 717 239; www.alternatura.hr) and Paiz (Vis town; 098 263 207)

King George III Fortress: open Jun–Sep: 10am–11pm daily; www.fortgeorge croatia.com

■ Trips to Biševo and the Blue Cave are organized by Alternatura (see left) and the Blue Cave Agency (Komiža; 021 713 752; www.visitbluecave.com).

■ Located diagonally opposite the Vis town ferry dock, Bejbi is a good spot for coffee or an evening drink.

■ The island is filled with military installations left by the British, Austrian and Yugoslav armed forces. Sign up for one of the military tours offered by local agents such as Alternatura or Paiz.

📻🔟 ⭐ Korčula Town

It's easy to see why the explorer Marco Polo would have been drawn to Korčula (even if it was not, as some suggest, his native town). There is no doubting the beauty of the place, a mosaic of terracotta rooftops encircled by medieval walls and punctuated by church spires, jutting out into the Adriatic with the majestic Pelješac mountains as a backdrop. Evidence of former Venetian rule abounds, from the proud lions adorning its buildings to a cathedral dedicated to St Mark.

1 City Walls

Korčula's city walls proved sturdy enough to see off an onslaught by the Ottoman Turks in 1571. Today large chunks of the fortifications have been cleared to make way for a road, although sections of wall do remain, with cannons peering out over the Pelješki Channel **(below)**, and a sprinkling of bastions still stand guard.

A scenic view of Korčula

MOREŠKA

Korčula is the only Dalmatian island where real swords are still used for dancing the Moreška (literally, "Moorish"). Dating from the 15th century, the dance has been performed in Korčula since the 16th century, and is believed to be a re-enactment of the victory of Christianity over Islam in Spain. Today's simplified form sees the White King (Christianity) fight the Black King (Islam), to set his fiancée, captured by the Black King, free. When the White King triumphs, the maiden is liberated.

2 Collection of Icons

Situated in a hall owned by the All Saints Brotherhood, Korčula's oldest fraternity, this collection features objects used in ceremonies and processions, as well as nine icons dating from the 14th–17th centuries, which were brought to Korčula from Crete.

3 Marco Polo House

Allegedly the great explorer's birthplace, this tower-like structure **(right)** was actually built several centuries after Marco Polo's time. It offers good views from the top floor.

4 Town Hall

The 16th-century town hall sits just inside the Land Gate. Its small loggia recalls Korčula town's Venetian heritage.

Previous pages Sculpture of a lion on the Cathedral of St Domnius, Split

Map of Korčula Town

9 Land Gate and Steps

The sweep of steps up to the Land Gate provides a dramatic entrance to the Old Town. Set in a 14th-century bastion, the gate was once a crucial strongpoint on the walls.

10 Cathedral of St Mark

This cathedral **(below)**, completed in the 15th century, is one of the most charming ecclesiastical buildings in the Adriatic islands. The interior is a wonderful riot of both Gothic and Renaissance styles.

6 Town Museum

Opposite the cathedral is a small civic museum, which is set in the striking 16th-century Gabriellis Palace. Among the exhibits is a copy of a 4th-century Greek tablet.

7 Marco Polo Exhibition

The life and times of the medieval globetrotter are recalled in this small display. Richly decorated tableaux, with lifelike costumed dummies, illustrate key moments from Polo's career.

5 Churches

Korčula town may be small, but it manages to cram in a wealth of churches. Look out for All Saint's Church, St Michael's and the Church of our Lady, which all stand within the Old Town walls.

8 Abbey Treasury

To the south of the cathedral stands the Abbey Treasury, with great works of art by Dubrovnik and Venetian artists, including masterpieces by Blaž Jurjev Trogiranin, Ivan Meštrović, Bassano and Carpaccio.

NEED TO KNOW

MAP E5 ■ Tourist Information: Obala dr. Franje Tuđmana 4. 020 715 701

Cathedral of St Mark: Trg Sv Marka; open 9am–7pm Mon–Sat; adm 25kn (combined ticket with Bishop's Palace)

Bishop's Palace: Trg Sv Marka; 020 711 049; open Jun–Aug: 9am–7pm Mon–Sat; Sep–May: by appt; adm

Civic Museum: Trg Sv Marka; 020 711 420; open Apr–Jun: 10am–2pm Mon–Sat; Jul–Sep: 9am–9pm Mon–Sat; Oct–Mar: 10am–1pm Mon–Sat; adm 20kn; children 6kn

Marco Polo House: Depolo; open Jul–Aug: 9am–9pm Mon–Sat; Apr–Jun & Sep–Oct: 9am–3pm; adm 20kn; children free

■ Housed in an old bastion, the popular bar Massimo *(see p82)* offers sweeping views out across the Pelješki Channel.

■ In high season, visit on Mondays and Thursdays to enjoy the Moreška *(see p63)*.

TOP 10 ⭐ Trogir

Trogir, a UNESCO World Heritage Site, is one of the most stunning places in the Mediterranean. Sitting on its own island with bridges linking it to the mainland on one side and Čiovo island on the other, the town forms a shimmering knot of orange roofs and traditional stone buildings, among which lies one of Croatia's most remarkable cathedrals. The well-preserved old centre is a pedestrianized oasis where the centuries peel back with every step.

1 Kamerlengo Fortress
This fortification **(below)** has guarded the western approaches to Trogir since the 15th century. Concerts and film screenings are held here in summer months.

2 Church of St John the Baptist
A small Romanesque church is all that remains of a great Benedictine monastery, the final resting-place of the Čipiko family. Their tomb is decorated with a 15th-century relief of *The Mourning of Christ*.

3 Loggia and Clock Tower
Traditionally a place where criminals were tried and shamed, the 14th-century loggia is notable for the conspicuous gap on its eastern wall, left when a Venetian stone lion was blown up by local activists in the 1930s.

4 Convent of St Nicholas
The art collection makes this modest convent worth visiting. The highlight, discovered in the 1920s, is the 3rd-century Greek relief of Kairos. Also note the chests used by new arrivals to the convent.

5 Cathedral of St Lawrence
Highlights include the 13th-century west door, lavishly adorned with biblical scenes carved by Trogir-born sculptor Radovan, and the Renaissance styling of the baptistry and St John's Chapel. Climb the tower **(left)** for views across Trogir and the surrounding coast.

6 Čipiko Palace
This Gothic edifice is one of the most impressive of the town's old palaces. It was once the base of the powerful 15th-century Čipiko family.

TROGIR ORIENTATION

Vehicles are banned from Trogir's historic core. However, visitors arriving by car can use the public car park located just outside the Old Town's northern walls; simply cross over the bridge from the mainland and turn right. Parking spaces are at a premium in summer, so many people opt to take the bus instead. The bus station is located not far from the aforementioned bridge, on the highway Jadranska Magistrala.

7 Civic Museum

Trogir's civic museum is housed in the Garagnin-Fanfogna Palace and presents details of the town's eclectic past. It houses everything from the legacy left by the Greeks and Romans to chilling documents from the Napoleonic era, listing the proclamation of death sentences on local officials who dared to defy French authority.

Map of Trogir

8 Riva

The waterfront Riva **(above)** is where locals and tourists come to wander or enjoy a meal or drink on balmy evenings. In season, boats line up here and visitors can book trips.

9 Land Gate

The most impressive surviving gate forms part of the fortifications built by the Venetians. A statue of St John, Trogir's patron saint, watches over new arrivals.

10 Marmont's Gazebo

During the Napoleonic era (1806–15) the governor of Napoleon's Illyrian Provinces, General Marmont, liked nothing better than to recline here **(left)**, taking in the views. It is still a striking spot, despite the nearby Čiovo shipyards.

NEED TO KNOW

MAP B3 ■ Tourist Information: Trg Ivana Pavla II 1; 021 885 628; www.visittrogir.hr

Cathedral of St Lawrence Bell Tower, Baptistry and Treasury: Trg Ivana Pavla II; 021 881 426; open Jun–Sep: 9am– 8pm daily; adm 15kn

Kamerlengo Fortress: open Apr–Oct: 8am– 10pm; adm 10kn

Civic Museum: Gradska vrata 4; 021 881 406; open Jun & Sep: 10am– 1pm, 5–8pm Mon–Sat; Jul & Aug: 10am–1pm, 6–9pm daily; Oct–May: 9am–2pm Mon–Fri; adm 20kn, children 15kn

Church of St John the Baptist: Trg Ivana Pavla II; May–Sep: 9am–7pm; Oct–Apr: by appt

Convent of St Nicholas: Gradska 2; open May– Sep: 10am–noon, 4–6:30pm daily; Oct– Apr: by appt; adm 5kn

■ The palm-fringed Riva is ideal for a relaxed coffee or meal. Try the Restoran Riva (see p93), open all year.

■ Cross the bridge to the island of Čiovo for great views across to the Old Town.

Diocletian's Palace, Split

Split's city centre is like no other in Europe. Built as a grand retirement home for Roman Emperor Diocletian, it was later modified by refugees from nearby Salona, who fled here when their own city was sacked in 614. It may be crumbling in parts, but the area occupied by the once mighty imperial palace – now a UNESCO World Heritage Site – has about 3,000 residents and is crammed with bars and boutique art shops. Unlike much of the Dalmatian coast, the whole complex buzzes with life all year round and offers a varied choice of things to see and do.

Peristyle ①
Once an ante-chamber to Diocletian's quarters, the dramatic, colonnaded square known as the Peristyle **(right)** is the heart of the palace complex.

ORIENTATION
From the waterfront Riva, Diocletian's Palace can be entered through the Bronze Gate. Head north through the main hall and go up the steps at the far end into the Peristyle, with its elegant colonnades and imposing cathedral. Just north of the cathedral is the city's most centrally located tourist office – a great place to pick up visitor information and maps. From the Peristyle, the main sights are easy to find – just a couple of minutes' walk north, east, west or south.

Ethnographic Museum ②
Located in labyrinthine alleys south of the Vestibule, this museum includes folk costumes and incorporates the medieval Chapel of St Andrew, former site of Diocletian's bedchamber.

Subterranean Chambers ③
The palace's underground vaults **(left)** mirror the layout of the imperial chambers that once stood above. They provide great insight into how the palace would have looked.

Cathedral of St Domnius ④
Built over Diocletian's tomb, the main structure here **(below)** is Roman. Inside are a 13th-century pulpit and work by 15th-century sculptor Juraj Dalmatinac.

6 Bell Tower

The bell tower, which soars high above the magnificent cathedral, was completed in the early 20th century. The panoramic views of the city that it offers **(left)** make the long climb worthwhile.

Plan of Diocletian's Palace

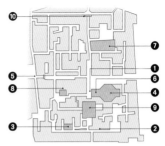

7 City Museum

East of the Peristyle, the City Museum is housed in the 15th-century Papalić Palace. Among the artifacts relating to Split's history, there is a great collection of weaponry and armour.

8 Baptistry

An alley opposite the cathedral leads to the Bapistry, once the Roman Temple of Jupiter. Inside, a striking feature is the sculpture of John the Baptist by Croatian sculptor Ivan Meštrović (1883–1962).

9 Vestibule

Stone steps from the Peristyle lead to this domed area **(below)**, where guests used to wait to see the Emperor. At night, stars are visible through a gap in the top.

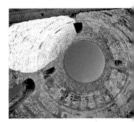

10 Golden Gate

This sturdy portal once led north to the nearby settlement of Salona. It has now been restored to its full splendour, thanks to funding by a local bank.

5 Iron Gate

The western entrance to the palace, the Iron Gate, was altered in the medieval era, when the 12th-century Church of Our Lady of the Belfry was built into its top storey. The belfry clock is thought to be the oldest surviving church tower on the Adriatic coast.

NEED TO KNOW

MAP M3 ▪ Tourist information: Peristyle; 021 345 606

Subterranean Chambers: Same as City Museum; adm 42kn; children 20kn

Cathedral of St Domnius: Peristyle; 021 345 602; open 8am–8pm Mon–Sat, noon–8pm Sun; adm 25kn

Bell Tower: Peristyle; open 8am–8pm Mon–Sat, noon–8pm Sun; adm 15kn

City Museum: Papalićeva 1; 021 360 171; open Apr–May: 8:30am–9pm daily, Jun–Sep: 8:30am–10pm daily, Oct: 8:30am–9pm Mon–Sat, 9am–5pm Sun, Nov–Mar: 9am–5pm Tue–Sat, 9am–2pm Sun; adm 22kn; children 10kn

▪ The spacious Luxor Café in the Peristyle is a good place to relax and refuel.

▪ Delve beyond the cupola to explore the upper tier of the palace. There are few major sights, but it is a lot quieter here, and there are good views of the Adriatic as well asa couple of lively bars at night.

Other Sights in Split

Aerial view of Marjan Hill and the Split waterfront

1 Marjan Hill
MAP L5

From the west side of the town, steps lead up to this stretch of greenery, part of a protected nature reserve. The views from the top are spectacular, with the mountains stretching off towards Bosnia in the distance and large swathes of the Dalmatian coast and its islands visible on a clear day.

2 Riva
MAP L2

Split's palm-fringed, pedestrianized waterfront is where its citizens come to meet up and be seen. The many pavement cafés make this the perfect spot to relax and gaze seawards at the ferries, as they slip off to the nearby islands.

3 Archeological Museum

The collections housed here (see p46) feature a variety of artifacts that date from the Roman, early Christian and medieval periods in Split, as well as a smaller legacy from the time of Greek rule in Dalmatia.

Relief, Archeological Museum

4 Meštrović Gallery

The Croatian-born, Expressionist sculptor Ivan Meštrović (1883–1962) may not have realized his dream of retiring to this impressive building (see p46), but it now provides a fitting home for a fine collection of his work.

5 Gallery of Fine Arts

Housed in a beautifully restored 18th-century hospital, Split's main art gallery (see p46) boasts one of the nation's best collections of Croatian art from the Renaissance onwards, as well as hosting some ground-breaking contemporary shows.

6 Fish Market
MAP L2

This wonderfully pungent and colourful market bursts into life every morning of the week. Here you can feast your eyes on the rich spread of Adriatic seafood, accompanied by a cacophony of gesticulating sellers and hollering locals.

7 Bačvice

A short walk southeast from the centre of Split leads to this small bay (see p92) with one of the city's most popular summer beaches. It is also home to a large waterfront entertainment centre filled with buzzing bars and nightclubs.

8 Trg Republike (Prokurative)
MAP L2

In contrast to the Roman parts of town, this square's grand architecture hints very clearly at Venetian origins.

9 Narodni Trg
MAP M2

When the Venetians rumbled into Split, they moved the focus of the city away from Diocletian's Palace, westwards and into this square. Highlights here are the 15th-century town hall and its grandiose ground-floor loggia.

10 Coastal Walk
MAP N6

The coastline stretching out from Bačvice is lined with beaches, cafés and nightclubs. East of here is a pretty coastal path leading past the tennis club where Wimbledon champion Goran Ivanišević launched his career.

EMPEROR DIOCLETIAN

Emperor Diocletian

Diocletian grew up in a family of modest means in the Dalmatian town of Salona, before embarking on a meteoric rise through the military ranks of the Roman Empire to assume the top position. He demonstrated a taste for grand construction projects; his greatest legacy to Croatia is the lavish retirement palace that he built by the Adriatic, and was later to evolve into the city of Split. Retirement was an unconventional move for a Roman emperor – his predecessors had all died on the job. From his grand seaside residence, Diocletian looked on as the Empire began to crumble, and it was here that he eventually took his own life. Given Diocletian's notoriety as a persecutor of Christians, it is ironic that Split's cathedral was later built on the site of his tomb.

**TOP 10
EVENTS IN
DIOCLETIAN'S LIFE**

1 AD 245: Diocletian is thought to have been born into a lowly Dalmatian family in Salona

2 282: Finds favour with Emperor Carus, and is made a Roman Count

3 283: Carus elevates his status to that of consul

4 284: Reaches his zenith, at the age of just 39, by becoming Roman Emperor

5 295: Commissions his seaside retirement palace in Split, which takes about a decade to complete

6 303: Outlaws Christianity, ordering the destruction of all churches and the persecution of Christians

7 305: Becomes the first Roman emperor to retire rather than die or be murdered on the job

8 308: Declines request to be reinstated as ruler of the Roman Empire

9 315: Diocletian's wife (Prisca) and daughter (Valeria) are murdered by Emperor Licinius

10 c.316: Poisons himself in his palace at Split

St George appears before Diocletian in this image from the late 13th-century manuscript *Scenes from the Life of St George*.

★ Hvar

This island just about has it all: from the swanky bars and yacht berths of Hvar town to UNESCO-protected Stari Grad Plain and family resort Jelsa, there's something for everyone. Despite its popularity, the island is by no means over-touristy, with an interior filled with bucolic villages and vineyard-covered hills, and a plethora of empty bays and coves, especially towards the island's eastern tip. The restaurants offer a blend of modern and traditional fare, and there's a growing roster of good local wines.

PETAR HEKTOROVIĆ'S TVRDALJ

One of Stari Grad's most famous buildings is the Tvrdalj, built as a family villa by Renaissance poet Petar Hektorović (1487–1572) and intended to symbolize his humanistic outlook on life. The Tvrdalj also served as a fortified refuge for townsfolk in the event of attack. Self-sufficiency was ensured by a walled garden, a pigeon loft in the main tower and a saltwater pond full of mullet – features that still survive today.

Hvar Town ②
An attractive huddle of villas, bars and boutiques set around a steep-rimmed bay, Hvar town **(right)** is for many the epitome of Adriatic chic. Popular with both the yachting crowd and younger party goers, it is also oozing with culture, boasting a set-piece Renaissance square, a historic theatre and a clutch of monasteries.

③ Milna
There's a string of beach locations east of Hvar town, of which the largely modern Milna is the most popular. It boasts rock and shingle beaches and is well equipped with cafés and restaurants.

Pakleni Islands ④
Taxi-boats leave from Hvar to these islands just off the coast. The largest, Jerolim, Marinkovac and Sveti Klement, are popular for day trips due to their shingle beaches **(right)** and restaurants.

① Hvar Fortress
Looking down on Hvar's port, this impressive fortress **(below)**, built in the 16th century, gives expansive views of the Pakleni islands. It's reached via an agave-lined zigzag walkway.

⑤ Vrboska
With buildings huddled on either side of an inlet spanned by a trio of bridges, Vrboska is famous for its traditional stone houses and the fortified, castle-like Church of St Mary that rises above the village.

⑥ Jelsa
A fishing port based around a parish, Jelsa has excellent beaches and promenades. With a clutch of pleasant hotels and campsites, too, it's a popular family destination in summer. Jelsa is also famous for its wineries.

7 Sućuraj

This mellow port at the east of the island is the departure point for ferries to Drvenik on the mainland and provides access to some relatively uncommercialized coves and beaches.

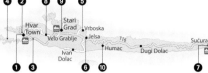

Map of Hvar Island

8 Velo Grablje

Set high in the hills between Hvar town and Stari Grad, Velo Grablje was the centre of the island's lavender-harvesting industry and remains a well-preserved example of a prosperous inland village, still complete with a village square, a church and traditional stone farmhouses.

9 Stari Grad

With its cobbled alleys, cute piazzas and colourful window-boxes, Stari Grad is one of the most soothing towns on the Adriatic coast. It is also one of the oldest towns in Europe. The UNESCO-protected Stari Grad Plain just east of town bears the pattern of field division that was adopted by Hvar's ancient Greek settlers.

10 Humac

Lying at the end of a windy road in the hills east of Jelsa, Humac is an atmospheric village of old houses and stone-paved streets, amid maquis and overgrown olive groves. The stalagmite- and stalactite-filled Grapčeva cave **(left)** is nearby.

NEED TO KNOW

MAP C4 ■ Tourist office (Hvar town): Trg svetog Stjepana 42; 021 741 059; www.tzhvar.hr ■ Tourist office (Stari Grad): Obala dr. Franje Tuđmana 1; 021 765 763; www.stari-grad.eu

Hvar Fortress: open Apr & May: 9am–8pm daily; Jun–Sep: 8am–11pm daily

Tvrdalj, Stari Grad: open Jun & Sep: 10am–1pm; Jul & Aug: 10am–1pm & 5–8pm daily

■ Only a short hop uphill from Hvar town's catamaran dock, Nonica *(see p82)* serves delicious pastries and cakes and is a quiet alternative to the crowded Riva cafés.

■ Car ferries run from Split to Stari Grad (three to six trips daily, depending on season) and from Drvenik to Sućuraj (five to ten times daily). Passenger-only catamarans run from Split and Dubrovnik to Hvar town twice a day during winter and more often otherwise, as well as from Vis to Hvar town on Tuesdays.

■ If you're travelling to or from Hvar with a car, be sure to arrive at the ferry dock in good time. Vehicles are loaded on a first-come, first-served basis, and late arrivals will have to wait for the next sailing.

TOP 10 ⭐ Pelješac Peninsula

A long, bony limb of land stretching west from the mainland north of Dubrovnik, the Pelješac Peninsula includes much that is distinctive about Dalmatian life. The red wine here is celebrated as the best in the country, and restaurants offer many traditional specialities, from locally farmed oysters to meats baked slowly in charcoal-covered pots. While the main town Orebić offers well-equipped hotels, the tourist scene is mostly informal, with beachside campsites and bay-hugging villages adding to the appeal.

PELJEŠAC WINES

Croatia's finest red wines are grown on Pelješac's south-facing coast, where sunlight, arid soil and salty sea breezes combine to produce small but fully flavoured grapes. The most popular variety is Plavac Mali, an indigenous grape that is related to Zinfandel and produces a heady, velvety red. Dingač and Postup are the most famous vineyard villages, and wine from either fetches a high price. All the local restaurants serve decent house wine, and there are plenty of specialist wineries offering the opportunity to taste and buy the best.

1 Mali Ston

This cluster of waterside houses **(left)** is famous for the oysters harvested in its enclosed, mainland-facing bay. A handful of excellent restaurants serve the local delicacy, drawing a year-round crowd of gourmet visitors.

2 Ston

Once a key fortress guarding the Republic of Ragusa's northern frontier, Ston stands at the western end of a stunning stretch of 14th-century walls. Running across the hillsides to link up with Mali Ston some 3 km (2 miles) away, the walls are open to visitors and offer sweeping views.

3 Orebić

This stately seaside town was famous for its 19th-century merchant fleet and still boasts the handsome villas and lush gardens **(right)** once owned by local ship captains. Orebić's long shingle beaches draw visitors from far and wide, and Korčula town is a short ferry ride across the Pelješki Channel.

4 Janjina

Occupying the high ground at Pelješac's narrowest point, Janjina offers a rare taste of rural Dalmatia. It is just a short walk downhill to the beaches of Drače, which face the mountainous mainland.

5 Dingač

Sheltering beneath craggy grey slopes, the seaside village of Dingač **(below)** is famous for the hillside-hugging vineyards that produce Croatia's best red wine. The grape harvest is notoriously difficult here due to the steep slopes.

Map of the Pelješac Peninsula

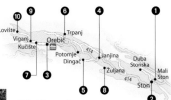

6 Trpanj

A quiet port backed by rugged mountains, Trpanj is the perfect base for exploring some of the off-the-beaten-track beaches of Pelješac's northern coast. Most celebrated of these is Divna, which lies at the end of a ravine to the west of town.

7 Kučište

A charming village featuring stone houses and small-boat piers sheltering beneath the slopes of Mount Sveti Ilija, Kučište is an ideal base for those who enjoy hill walking and mountain-biking.

8 Žuljana

Squeezed into a south-facing cove at the end of a crooked ravine, the cute fishing village of Žuljana boasts one of Pelješac's finest shingle beaches. It is also a diver's paradise.

9 Viganj

The stiff breezes of the Pelješac Channel have helped Viganj become the prime windsurfing resort in Croatia **(right)**. Most of the surfers stay in one of Viganj's numerous campsites, and there is a fine shingle beach for those who prefer to take it easy and spend time lying in the sun.

NEED TO KNOW

MAP F5 ■ Tourist office: Trg Mimbeli, Orebić; 020 713 718; www.visitorebic-croatia.hr

Car hire and travel agent: Orebić Tours, Ulica Bana Jelačića 84, Orebić; 020 713 367; www.orebic-tours.hr

■ Café Croccantino, just around the corner from the Orebić ferry dock, is rightly celebrated for its ice cream and cakes – perfect for a quick treat before crossing the Channel to Korčula.

■ There is limited public transport on the peninsula, so you really need a car to explore. Hire one in Dubrovnik or from a local agent in Orebić.

10 Lovište

A sleepy fishing village stretching along a broad shallow bay, Lovište is the perfect place to wind down and relax. Several evocative, abandoned villages on the shoulders of Mount Sveti Ilija lie just inland.

The Top 10 of Everything

The idyllic bay at Milna, on the southwest coast of Hvar Island

🔟 Moments in History

① 4th Century BC: Greeks and Illyrians in Dalmatia

Greek settlers began to cross the seas and join the Illyrian tribes who had already been eking out a living on the Dalmatian coastline. As the population along the coastal strip expanded, trade links and proto-settlements started to flourish.

② 1st Century AD: Romans Move into Dalmatia

The Roman Empire surged east, engulfing swathes of Croatia and snuffing out most of the indigenous opposition. Wine production flourished as the conquerors brought their skills to a land whose soil and climate made it perfect for producing both red and white wines.

③ 6th Century AD: Arrival of Slavic Tribes

Slavic tribes from the north began to arrive on the Dalmatian coast.

④ AD 925: Alleged First Croatian King Crowned

Croatia became a nation under King Tomislav, the "Father of the Croats", who united the country for the first time. Croatia's independence, however, was soon quashed by the power of the Huns and the mighty Venetian doges. The latter soon wielded greater influence over Dalmatia.

⑤ 1409: Dalmatia Comes Under Venetian Control

King Ladislaus of Naples sold Dalmatia to the Venetian Republic for 100,000 ducats, but Dubrovnik retained its independence from both Venice and the Ottoman Empire.

Statue of King Tomislav

⑥ 1808: Napoleon Annexes Republic of Ragusa

In 1806, French troops saved Dubrovnik from a month-long siege by Russian and Montenegrin forces. Two years later, Napoleon claimed Ragusa for France.

Portrait of Napoleon Bonaparte

⑦ 1815: Dalmatia Comes Under Habsburg Rule

After a period of Napoleonic French control, Dalmatia and Dubrovnik were awarded to the Habsburg Empire by the Congress of Vienna. Under Austrian rule, Dalmatia remained economically undeveloped, but tourism grew towards the end of the 19th century.

⑧ 1918: First Yugoslav State Created in the Wake of World War I

With the fall of the Habsburg Empire at the end of World War I, Croatian politicians voted to join the new Kingdom of Serbs, Croats and Slovenes (later renamed Yugoslavia). Croats expected a degree of national autonomy and were disappointed when the union created a Serb-dominated state centred on Belgrade.

Josip Broz Tito

⑨ 1945: Tito Comes to Power

Croatian-born communist Josip Broz Tito built the Partisan movement in World War II and re-established Yugoslavia after the war. He created a federation in which Serbs, Croats, Slovenes, Montenegrins, Bosnians and Macedonians each had their own republic. Tito's Yugoslavia was thrown out of the Soviet bloc in 1948, improving relations with the West.

War after Croatian independence

⑩ 1991: Croatia Declares its Independence

A landslide referendum saw Croatia gain independence from Yugoslavia. Irregular Serbian units, backed up by the Yugoslav military, attacked the republic and besieged Dubrovnik. Hostilities had ceased by the end of 1995, and all captured Croatian territory was returned by 1998.

TOP 10 HISTORICAL FIGURES

1 Emperor Diocletian
Diocletian (245–316) built a retirement palace on the Adriatic coast, founding Split in the process *(see p30)*.

2 King Tomislav
Allegedly crowned in c.925, Tomislav was one of the first rulers to unite Adriatic and inland Croatia in the same state.

3 Grgur of Nin
This 10th-century bishop campaigned for the use of the Croatian language (rather than Latin) in church services.

4 Matija Ivanić
The Hvar merchant (1445–1523) led a rebellion against aristocratic Venetian rule and is still considered a folk hero.

5 Antun Rozanović
When Ottoman corsair Uluz Ali raided the Dalmatian islands in 1571, priest Rozanović led the defence of Korčula and saved the town.

6 Marshal Auguste de Marmont
Napoleon's progressive Governor of Dalmatia (1806–11) promoted reforms and built roads.

7 Nikola Tesla
Raised in Dalmatia before moving to the USA, Tesla (1856–1943) was one of the most gifted inventors of modern times.

8 Ante Pavelić
Fascist leader Pavelić (1889–1959) served as puppet ruler of Axis-occupied Croatia from 1941 to 1945. His rule provoked one of Europe's biggest anti-fascist uprisings.

9 Marshal Josip Broz Tito
Tito (1892–1980) fought the Axis forces before leading Yugoslavia after World War II.

10 Franjo Tuđman
Tuđman (1922–99) became the first president of the newly independent Croatia in 1991.

Franjo Tuđman

🔟 Old Towns

A corner of magical Trogir

Greeks in 384 BC. Central Stari Grad's narrow alleys have an air of antiquity, although most of the stone houses date from medieval or Renaissance times. The fortified Tvrdalj, or villa, of poet Petar Hektorović offers an insight into the lifestyles of 16th-century Hvar nobles.

1 Trogir

Set picturesquely on an islet between the mainland and the island of Čiovo, this grand creation (see pp28–9) can make a credible claim for the title of finest old town on the Adriatic coast. Trogir's unity of design makes it special, which is why the locals call it the "town museum".

2 Stari Grad (Hvar)

Stari Grad – literally "Old Town" – is a fitting name for this settlement (see p77) founded by

3 Dubrovnik

Lord Byron's "Pearl of the Adriatic" is Croatia's most famous set-piece. Encapsulated within the hulking medieval walls is a perfectly preserved Baroque city-state (see pp12–19), sandwiched between a sweep of limestone mountains to the north and the Adriatic to the south. Now rediscovered by tourists, the Old City (see pp66–75) can often get crowded in summer, but there's no disguising its allure.

4 Hvar Town

It is easy to see why Hvar town (see p77) is the summer getaway of choice for Croatia's cognoscenti. The charming old core, crammed with Venetian architecture, sweeps around a wide Adriatic bay. High above, a rambling fort watches over the summer scene of pavement

Hvar town's bustling harbour in summer

8 Ston

The historic salt-manufacturing town of Ston (see p95) was bought by the city of Dubrovnik in 1335, becoming a key fortress on the northern border of the republic. The town walls, running from Ston to the port of Mali Ston, 3 km (2 miles) east, are among the best preserved in mainland Europe. The uniform grid pattern of the town attests to the order and proportion for which Dubrovnik's urban planners were once famed.

cafés, fish restaurants and bobbing tour boats. The main square is dominated by the contours of the Cathedral of St Stephen (see p45).

5 Split

No staid museum piece, Split's Old Town (see pp30–33) is a living and breathing slice of history, formed around the confines of the Emperor Diocletian's palatial water-front retirement home, and adapted over the centuries by the Splicani.

6 Kut (Vis)

Relatively few visitors have discovered the historic Kut district of Vis town (see p22), with its out-standing Renaissance triple-naved church, Our Lady of Spilica, its swathe of old Venetian merchant dwellings, and its trio of first-rate restaurants. In the ramble of narrow lanes near the waterfront, old women hang out their washing from balconies that were built by wealthy Venetians, while the local cats look on.

7 Komiža (Vis)

Set around a bay on the western shores of Vis, Komiža (see p79) is a medieval fishing port that has changed little through the centuries. Stout houses adorned with family crests huddle around narrow streets and tiny piazzas, while a spectacular pair of sumptuously decorated churches are testament to Komiža's erstwhile wealth as the centre of the Adriatic anchovy-processing business.

9 Lastovo Town
MAP D6

Unusually, Lastovo town (see p97) turns its back on the Adriatic and tumbles in the opposite direction. Less ornate than many other Dalmatian towns, its most striking buildings are a group of 20 or so Renaissance stone houses, charac-terized by their high, broad terraces.

The rooftops of Korčula town

10 Korčula Town

This mini-Dubrovnik (see p78) matches its more illustrious sibling in everything but scale. Enjoying its own rocky promontory, this old town (see pp26–7), carved over the centu-ries by the Venetians, still feels like an oasis not yet well acquainted with the 20th century, let alone the 21st. Within its walls lie churches, seafood eateries, and the site where, locals believe, their most famous inhabi-tant, Marco Polo, was born.

🔟 Cathedrals and Churches

The Church of Our Lady of the Rocks, situated on the island of Lopud

1 Our Lady of the Rocks, Lopud

MAP G6

Some of the Dubrovnik region's best Renaissance artworks are inside this parish church on a promontory above the ferry dock. Overlooking the altar is a three-panel *Virgin and Child* painting by Dubrovnik master Nikola Božidarević. The altar screen is a masterpiece of stone carving.

2 Cathedral of St Mark, Korčula

An outstanding example of late medieval architecture, Korčula's Cathedral of St Mark *(see p27)* dominates the Old Town from the peninsula's highest point. Its distinctive tower is topped by an octagonal cupola; below, the façade boasts late Gothic details, notably the grotesque Adam and Eve squatting over the main door. The interior features a splendid altar painting by Tintoretto of saints Mark, Bartholomew and Jerome.

3 Our Lady of the Pirates, Komiža

MAP B5

Perched serenely above the main family beach at the northern end of Komiža's waterfront, this is one of Dalmatia's most unusual churches. It has three naves of almost equal size, each with its own high altar. Legend has it that a painting of the Virgin was stolen from the church by pirates, only to return washed up on the beach when the thieves were shipwrecked in a divine storm.

4 Our Lady of the Snows, Cavtat

MAP H7

Another church with an unusual name – referring to a miraculous snow storm that occurred early one August – this former monastery church stands at the end of Cavtat's palm-fringed harbour. Inside, Božidar Vlatković's *Virgin and Child* (1494) hangs above the main altar, while a Viktor

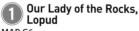

Dobričević polyptych at the back of the church portrays saints Michael, Nicholas and John the Baptist. The church is the focus of festivities on 5 August, with religious processions involving the whole town.

5 Dubrovnik Cathedral

Legend has it that Dubrovnik Cathedral (see pp66–7) was founded by Richard the Lionheart in gratitude for his life being spared during a violent storm that washed him up on the island of Lokrum. One of the country's most striking religious buildings, its treasures include Baroque frescoes, Byzantine skull case of St Blaise, and *Ascension* by Titian.

Statue at the Church of St Blaise, Dubrovnik

6 Cathedral of St Lawrence, Trogir

The 13th-century west portal by local master Radovan is the *pièce de résistance* of this remarkable cathedral (see pp28–9). Look out for the figures of Adam and Eve on either side, standing proudly over a pair of Venetian lions (indicating the influence Venice once had over Trogir). Arranged around the upper sections of the portal are depictions of the saints and scenes of local life.

Cathedral of St Lawrence, Trogir

7 Church of St Blaise, Dubrovnik

Dubrovnik's revered patron saint, St Blaise (see p15), is said to have saved the city from sacking by the Venetians. He pops up throughout the city but is perhaps most pleasingly represented in this 18th-century church.

8 Orthodox Church, Dubrovnik
MAP F9

Dubrovnik has been home to an Orthodox Christian community for many centuries, and this is their main place of worship in the Old City. Set behind wrought-iron railings, the church was built in Neo-Byzantine style, with squat rectangular belfries protruding from its ornate façade. Inside, a carved wooden icon screen is studded with portraits of saints. The church's collection of medieval icons, prayer books, and 19th-century portraits by local painter Vlaho Bukovac is housed in a small museum next door.

9 Cathedral of St Stephen, Hvar Town
MAP C4

Be sure to pop in here if you get lucky with its erratic opening hours. The 16th-century Renaissance building stands on the site of an old Benedictine monastery. One highlight is the altar's understated 13th-century *Madonna and Child*.

10 Mušter, Komiža
MAP B5

Set amid vines on a steep bluff overlooking the sleepy fishing town of Komiža, the Mušter is a fortified former monastery with jutting bastions and a stout defensive tower. The monastery church, dedicated to fishermen's patron St Nicholas, contains splendid Baroque altars.

🔟 Museums and Galleries

1 Gallery of Fine Arts, Split
MAP N1 ▪ Ulica kralja Tomislava 15 ▪ 021 350 110 ▪ Open 10am–6pm Tue–Fri, 10am–2pm Sat & Sun ▪ www.galum.hr ▪ Adm

This major collection covers Croatian art through the ages. Look out for masterful portraits by Vlaho Bukovac (1855–1922) and moody cityscapes by Emanuel Vidović (1870–1953)

Gallery of Fine Arts, Split

2 Archeological Collection Issa, Vis Town
MAP B5 ▪ Viški boj 12 ▪ 021 329 340 ▪ Open Jun–Sep: 9am–1pm & 5–7pm daily; Oct–May: by appt ▪ Adm

Sculptures, ceramics, weapons and everyday items illuminate life in the Ancient Greek town of Issa (modern Vis town).

3 The Island of Brač Museum, Škrip
MAP C3 ▪ 021 637 092 ▪ Open 8am–8pm daily ▪ Adm

Treasures from all over Brač are housed in the Radojković Tower, which shows traces of Illyrian, Roman and early Croatian architecture.

4 Archeological Museum, Split
MAP M5 ▪ Zrinsko-Frankopanska 25 ▪ 021 329 340 ▪ Open Jun–Sep: 9am–2pm & 4–8pm Mon–Sat; Oct–May: 9am–2pm & 4–8pm Mon–Fri, 9am–2pm Sat ▪ Adm

Exhibits at this museum include Ancient Greek ceramics, weaponry from the 6th to 9th centuries, over 70,000 coins, and amphorae recovered from shipwrecks.

5 Branislav Dešković Gallery, Bol
MAP C4 ▪ Porat bolskih pomoraca 7 ▪ 021 637 092 ▪ Open mid-Jun–mid-Sep: 9am–noon & 6–11pm Tue–Sun; mid-Sep–mid-Jun: 9am–3pm Tue–Sat ▪ Adm ▪ www.czk-brac.hr

This small gallery on the Adriatic coast displays local artists, as well as those from other parts of Croatia. Of particular interest is the career-spanning collection of works by Expressionist Ignjat Job (1895–1936).

6 Maritime Museum, Dubrovnik
The most interesting part of the collection (see p13) illustrates Dubrovnik's naval might between the 12th and 14th centuries, when it threatened Venice's supremacy.

7 Meštrović Gallery, Split
MAP L6 ▪ Šetalište Ivana Meštrovića 46 ▪ 021 340 800 ▪ Open May–Sep: 9am–7pm Tue–Sun; Oct–Apr: 9am–4pm Tue–Sat, 10am–3pm Sun ▪ Adm

More than 80 of Ivan Meštrović's sculptures, including a huge *Pietà* and bronze, marble, plaster and wood works, can today be viewed at his former home. The dining room contains the sculptor's furniture and family portraits.

Meštrović Gallery, Split

Exterior of the Hermitage of Blaca

8 Hermitage of Blaca, Brač

MAP C4

This 16th-century monastery and its contents, including correspondence between the last priest and the Royal Astronomical Society in London, have been frozen in time since 1963. A stunning location and roaming goats enhance its appeal. Access is on foot.

9 Kuća Bukovac, Cavtat

MAP H7 ▪ Bukovčeva 5 ▪ 020 478 646 ▪ Open Apr–Oct: 9am–6pm, Mon–Sat, 9am–2pm Sun; Nov–Mar: 10am–6pm Tue–Sat, 9am–1pm Sun ▪ Adm

The famous Croatian painter Vlaho Bukovac was born here. It retains the qualities of a typical 19th-century bourgeois home and is now a museum with his paintings on display.

10 Stari Grad Museum, Stari Grad

MAP C4 ▪ Ulica braće Biankini 4 ▪ 021 766 324 ▪ Open Jul & Aug: 10am–1pm & 7–9pm Mon–Sat, 7–9pm Sun; May, Jun, Sep & Oct: 10am–1pm Mon–Sat ▪ Adm

This museum is worth visiting for the building alone – a family villa with many of its Neo-Renaissance features intact. Local artists Bartul Petrić (1899–1974) and Juraj Plančić (1899–1930) have a whole floor to themselves. It also houses an interesting archaeological collection.

TOP 10 PUBLIC MONUMENTS

1 Orson Welles, Split
The Hollywood actor-director spent a lot of time in Split, a connection honoured by the monument sculpted by his Croatia-born partner Oja Kodar.

2 Father Andrija Kačić Miošić, Makarska
Impressive tribute to this 18th-century priest and poet.

3 Marko Marulić, Split
Meštrović's homage to the Split-born writer (1450–1524) often dubbed "the father of Croatian Literature".

4 The Seagull, Makarska
This seafront sculpture of a local lad romancing a foreign girl is a nod to the Dalmatian reputation for flirting

5 Orlando's Column, Dubrovnik
Standard-bearer for the Divine Republic, Orlando flies the Libertas flag of the Dubrovnik Festival in summer *(see p14)*.

6 Ivan Gundulić, Dubrovnik
Oversized Meštrović statue, honouring the life and work of this local 17th-century poet.

7 Dr Franjo Tuđman, Split
Croatia's first president is shown in thoughtful mode in a dignified statue at the entrance to Split harbour.

8 Nikola Duboković, Jelsa, Hvar
Cast by the great Ivan Rendić, this monument to a local seafarer is one of Dalmatia's finest public sculptures.

9 The New Riva, Split
The westward extension of the seafront Riva has metal plaques that mark the achievements of local sportspeople.

10 Grgur Ninski, Split
A colossal image of Gregory of Nin, who campaigned for Mass to be conducted in Croatian.

Statue of Grgur Ninski in Split

Beaches

golf-cart taxi for a small fee. A lively bar at the back of the beach provides refreshments.

 **Zlatni Rat, Brač**
MAP C4

The "Golden Cape"– a popular sweep of fine shingle that curls out, lapped by the currents of the Adriatic, from the pine-fringed southern flank of the island of Brač – is much eulogized, and photos of this distinctive landmark near the resort of Bol are, rightly, omnipresent in holiday brochures.

1 Banje Beach, Dubrovnik
MAP K9

The sand may be imported, and there's an entry charge to the section with sun loungers, but the sweeping views of old Dubrovnik and the island of Lokrum are hard to beat, and the waters are exceptionally clean.

Banje beach, Dubrovnik

2 Šunj, Lopud
A bay-enclosed crescent of fine shingle at the eastern end of Lopud island, Šunj *(see p99)* is one of the finest beaches in the Dubrovnik region, but it is rarely overcrowded due to its island location. The 40-minute walk from the Lopud ferry dock takes you through a wonderful Mediterranean landscape of olive groves, drystone walls and maquis. If you don't feel like walking, take a

4 Kamenica, Komiža, Vis
MAP B5

There are several pebbly coves immediately south of Komiža, and Kamenica is the largest and best equipped. It spreads beneath a sandy bluff covered with agaves and other Mediterranean flora. Kamenica's beach bar is a party destination that draws a young crowd on summer nights. The dog-friendly smaller bay just north of Kamenica is ideal for those with a canine companion.

5 Milna, Hvar
MAP C4

Hvar town lacks long uninterrupted stretches of beach, so many visitors make their way to Milna, which is 3 km (2 miles) east. Stone slabs and rocks abut the sea at the centre of the village, and there's a fine shingle beach a short walk to the west. There are several good restaurants above the beaches, and Milna offers plenty of parking space.

6 Trstenica, Orebić
You couldn't wish for a more spectacular location to unfurl your towel than the Trstenica beach *(see p99)* at this small resort, with its collage of fine shingle and sand.

Trstenica beach, Orebić

Across the water, on the nearby island of Korčula, you can see the terracotta roof tiles of Korčula town, as starched mountain-scapes embrace all around.

7 Pržina Bay, Lumbarda
MAP E5

While chocolate-box beauty Korčula town gets all the plaudits, the nearby town of Lumbarda has much better beaches. Pržina Bay has a decent sandy beach with a sprinkling of cafés in a very low-key scene. Buses run daily from Korčula town, while in summer there are boats as well. If Pržina Bay gets a little too crowded for your liking, nearby Bilin Žal tends to be a bit quieter.

8 Proizd, Vela Luka, Korčula
MAP C5

Bathing spots don't get much more dramatic than Proizd, a rocky island just off the western coast of Korčula, accessible by taxi-boat from Vela Luka. Proizd's popularity rests on the huge slabs of rock that slope steeply into clear seas on its northern side, providing perfect perches on which to catch the sun's rays. A restaurant and café are also close at hand.

9 Gradac

The small town of Gradac (see p88) boasts the longest beach in Croatia, and the best on the Makarska Riviera. Shingle and pebbles abound along the tree-fringed shoreline. Out to sea, the island of Hvar looms on the horizon. Some sections of the beach offer tourist facilities; others are far more rustic. In summer it can be tricky to find a secluded spot.

10 Pakleni Islands
MAP B4–C4

This necklace of tiny islands just off Hvar provides plenty of great places to laze by the sea. The name derives from the pine resin, *paklina*, once used to waterproof boats. A short boat trip from Hvar town and you find yourself sitting by the Adriatic with very little in the way of tourist development to spoil the surroundings. Clothes are very much optional on Jerolim.

A beach on the Pakleni Islands

🔟 Sailing Routes

The beautiful waters between Dubrovnik and Korčula

1 Dubrovnik–Korčula

This southern-Adriatic route eases its way from Dubrovnik *(see pp66–75)* to Koločep, Lopud, Šipan and Mljet *(see p97)*. From the Mljet National Park, head up the Pelješki Channel en route to Korčula town *(see pp26–7)*. A detour from Šipan to Ston, from where you can walk to Mali Ston *(see p96)* and savour Adriatic fish, is well worth it.

2 Split–Dugi Otok

This stunning but less well-trodden route takes sailors from Split *(see pp30–33)* to Šolta *(see p79)*, Rogoznica and Žirje, then into the Kornati Islands archipelago, where Piškera has a good marina. From here, journey to Dugi Otok before returning via Primošten, which has become quite a hub for sailors over the years.

3 Trogir–Lastovo

Watch enviously from Trogir marina *(see pp28–9)* as the millionaires moor up on the Riva before heading due south to Brač *(see pp78–9)*, Hvar *(see pp34–5)*, Korčula *(see pp26–7)* and Lastovo *(see p97)*. For a real Robinson Crusoe experience, explore the islets to the northeast – Češvinica, Kručica, Stomorina and Saplun. Saplun has the added bonus of sand beaches.

4 Vis–Korčula, via Hvar

The direct route from Vis to Korčula runs through open sea; it's far more interesting to take this two- to three-day detour via Hvar town, the mysterious southern coast of Hvar island, and the beautiful uninhabited Šćedro island.

5 Split–Vis

Many yachts make a beeline for Brač and Hvar, and miss out on the beauty of Šolta (much favoured by the Splićani) and Vis. Hvar certainly has its attractions, though – not least of which are the plentiful secluded coves that are flanked by impressive mountains.

6 Bays and Beaches of Pelješac and Korčula

Start and finish in Korčula by taking this three-day circuit of southern Dalmatia's best beaches, working your way around the south of Korčula

Aerial view of the Pelješac beach

via Bačva Bay and Pupnatska Luka, returning by way of the southern coast of Pelješac.

7 Vis to the Outer Islands

Komiža is a good starting point for a two- to three-day tour of Croatia's westernmost islands, with the grey volcanic cone of Jabuka and lighthouse-topped ridge of Palagruža particularly alluring. The nearest island to Komiža, Biševo, has fine beaches and some seasonal taverns.

8 Trogir–Dubrovnik

Be warned: this is a trip for serious sailing enthusiasts, with big distances between stops. Starting from Trogir, the route takes in Hvar, Vis, Vela Luka (Korčula), Mljet and Dubrovnik.

The Riva at Trogir

9 Split–Dubrovnik

An extended one-way charter allows a thorough exploration of central and southern Dalmatia, taking in Split, Trogir, Šolta, Brač, Hvar, Vis, Korčula, Mljet and Dubrovnik. Take the time to explore islands and islets, such as Pakleni Otoci *(see p49)* and the islands around Mljet's Polače Bay. This route also allows an exploration of more than one settlement on each island.

10 Trogir–Trogir

A two- to three-day trip out of Trogir takes you to the semi-wild beaches of Drvenik Mali and Veli and alluring Šešula inlet on the western flanks of Šolta, before returning via the eastern coast of Čiovo.

TOP 10 SAILING TIPS

Charter yacht off Dalmatia

1 Know the Rules
Before sailing, check the local rules at the local port or tourist office.

2 Join a Flotilla
Consider joining a flotilla; shorter distances and tuition make them ideal for beginners.

3 Reputable Operators
www.adriaticholidays.co.uk
▪ www.sunsail.eu ▪ www.cosmos yachting.com
Adriatic Holidays, Sunsail and Cosmos Yachting are all established businesses.

4 Charter a Skipper
He or she will know the waters very well indeed, and may even cook.

5 Vital Documentation
Make sure you have certified crew and passenger lists, as well as proof that the boat is seaworthy and has third-party insurance, and that you are authorized to sail it.

6 Pre-book Marinas
From June to September, mooring space is at a premium.

7 Sail During the "Shoulder" Season
For good weather without the summer crowds, May and September are best.

8 Weather Forecasts
Check the weather on your VHF radio. For Dubrovnik the frequency is 73; for Split it is 67.

9 Pack Sparingly
It's surprising how many beginners try to fit six huge suitcases on board; remember that space is at a premium.

10 Annual Berths
www.aci-marinas.com
If you intend to berth your boat in Croatia long-term, consider joining the ACI (Adriatic Croatia International Club).

🔟 Outdoor Activities

Windsurfing off the Dalmatian coast

① Windsurfing
Big Blue Sport: www.big-blue-sport.hr

Windswept coastlines on Brač and along the Pelješki Channel (Korčula and Pelješac) are all popular haunts for windsurfers.

② Rafting
Kentona: www.rafting-cetina.com

Adrenaline-fuelled white-water rafting trips are becoming increasingly popular, with a number of operators organizing trips on the Cetina river. Trips generally last from 3 to 4 hours, and take place on the lower stretch of this 105-km-(65-mile-) long waterway, around 20 minutes from the coastal town of Omiš (see p89).

③ Walking and Hiking
Headwater: www.headwater.com

Dalmatia has an almost infinite number of walking and hiking opportunities, from easy, low-level walks to steep ascents requiring a higher level of fitness. Seek local advice, and ensure that you have the right equipment. UK-based Headwater organize walking holidays around the Dalmatian coast.

④ Tennis

National heroes Goran Ivanišević, Iva Majoli and Mario Ančić have all fuelled Croatia's love of tennis. Public courts can be found near resort hotels and towns throughout Dalmatia. One of the region's most famous courts is in Bačvice (see p32), Split, where Ivanišević trained as a youngster.

⑤ Scuba Diving
Croatian Diving Federation: www.diving-hrs.hr

Dive schools along the Dalmatian coast offer trial dives, diving courses, equipment hire, night dives and wreck dives. Some of the best diving can be done with Biševo's Blue Cave from the island of Vis, where there are myriad offshore wrecks. Contact the Croatian Diving Federation for more information.

⑥ Climbing

The vaulting peaks of the Biokovo mountain ranges have an irresistible allure to mountaineers, who flock here from all over Europe. There are also numerous climbing routes on the cliffs and canyons surrounding Split. Organized tours with qualified instructors advise climbers of all abilities.

Rock climbing near Split

7 Swimming

Given Croatia's lengthy coastline, it's hardly surprising that swimming is a popular outdoor sport. Those not keen to swim in the sea will find enclosed pools near the waterfronts in Korčula and Split, among others.

8 Sea Kayaking

This is a sport that experts expect to take off in a big way over the coming years, with the majority of trips centred around Dubrovnik and the Elafiti Islands. You can take anything from a short excursion to a week-long break. Local travel agencies in Dubrovnik can organize sea-kayaking tours.

Sea kayaking by Dubrovnik Old City

9 Snorkelling

It is cheap and easy, with a bountiful coastline to choose from; just don a mask and flippers, and you're away.

10 Picigin, Split

A summer sport peculiar to Split, picigin is more about posing than point-scoring. Head to Bačvice (see p32), stand in the sea with a small black rubber ball, wearing your best swimwear and designer sunglasses, throw the ball nonchalantly then catch it with one hand, and you will blend in perfectly with the Splićani.

TOP 10 SPECTATOR SPORTS

An Italy–Croatia football match

1 Football
Dalmatians are passionate about football. Football shirts and the graffiti of their fans (known as the Torcida) attest to the fact that most support premier-division Hajduk Split.

2 Basketball
Dalmatia's most famous stars, Dražen Petrović and Krešimir Ćosić (now both sadly deceased), fuelled the nation's dedication to the sport.

3 Tennis
Croatia has its own home-grown tennis celebrities, so Croatians like to watch the game as much as they like to play it.

4 Sailing
Regular regattas and boat shows have made sailing more than just a participant sport.

5 Beach Volleyball
In peak season, beach volleyball matches spring up along the Makarska Riviera.

6 Water Polo
A strong national team has secured water polo a sizable following.

7 Athletics
Croatians like watching athletics. Split-born Blanka Vlašić is a two-time world champion in high jump and has two Olympic medals, silver and bronze

8 Cycling
Brač hosts the Uvati Vitar, a three-day bike marathon in May. The Tour of Croatia, a popular men's cycling race, has one of its stages in Dalmatia.

9 Handball
Handball surged in popularity when Croatia won gold at the 2004 Olympics.

10 Rowing
The Skelin brothers from Split took silver at the 2004 Olympics. Most Dalmatian towns have a rowing club.

🔟 Children's Dalmatia

Exploring the city walls in Dubrovnik is a great family day out

1 Fortifications and Towers

Dalmatia overflows with towers and fortifications offering stunning views. Lather on the sunscreen and carry plenty of water. Cafés located along the way help ease the strain for shorter legs, often offering high vantage points at the top of towers and in the fortifications themselves.

2 Aquaparks

An increasingly common feature of Dalmatia's beach resorts is the aquapark made up of inflatable blocks, ramps and walkways, allowing children to slide and splash around in shallow waters under the watchful eye of supervisors. There's usually an entrance fee, and lifebelts are provided. Well-equipped aquaparks can be found at Bol (see p78) and at Soline beach, near Vrboska (see p80).

3 Outdoor Cinemas

This traditional feature of Dalmatian life has been revived in recent years, with the renovation and reopening of seaside cinemas. As well as fresh maritime breezes al fresco screens in Dubrovnik, Bol, Supetar, Split, Vis, Hvar, and some other towns offer up-to-date choice of movies including options for family and children, which usually start early in the evening.

4 Public Swimming Pools

They may not be plush, but Dalmatia has some of the best-located public swimming pools in Europe, allowing parents to enjoy views of places such as Korčula Old Town, the island of Šolta (from Split) and the bay at Šibenik while the kids take a dip.

5 Playparks

Every Dalmatian town has a traditional playpark with swings, slides and climbing frames. Among the best equipped are those behind the main beach in Makarska (see p87) and on the south side of Gruž harbour in Dubrovnik.

6 Adventure Sports

If your older children crave a little excitement, adrenaline-pumping white-water rafting, sea

River rafting on the Cetina river

kayaking, river canoeing, sailing, mountain biking and organized hiking trips can be arranged at local travel agencies.

7 Ferries

The whole length of the Dalmatian coast is awash with catamarans and ferries of all shapes and sizes, transforming a sightseeing visit to an island into a sea-borne adventure. It's best to leave the car behind at the height of the summer.

8 Resort Hotels

The swimming pools, tennis courts and other leisure facilities at resort-style hotels will keep kids happily occupied for hours. Full- and half-board options are worth considering, particularly with younger children.

Child-friendly Amfora Resort, Hvar

9 Cycling

Once you get away from the busy highways and tourist resorts, Dalmatia is replete with cycling opportunities. Many hotels and camp-sites provide or rent bikes to guests. Bicycle seats for young children are almost always available.

10 Beaches

Sandy beaches may be few and far between, but Dalmatia boasts long stretches of clean, sun-kissed pebble and shingle beach. Even at the height of summer, you will find whole swathes of shoreline deserted. On busy public beaches, snack bars, sun loungers and parasols are common – some have changing rooms and showers.

TOP 10 CHILDREN'S ATTRACTIONS

Windsurfing at Zlatni Rat Beach

1 Zlatni Rat, Bol
This is one of Dalmatia's best family beaches, with windsurfing, kayaking and an inflatable aquapark nearby.

2 Croatia's "Dead Sea" Lake
Children are delighted to find they can float with ease in the salt waters of the Mrtvo More, a sea-fed lake on the island of Lokrum (see p20).

3 Biševo's Blue Cave
On a sunny day, children will find this spot mesmerising (see p23).

4 Beach Activities, Hvar
The beach just outside the Amfora Resort is a good place to hire snorkelling equipment and mountain bikes.

5 Spanish Fort, Hvar Town
This 16th-century fort is a firm favourite with all ages, and the young ones can burn off some energy on the steep ascent.

6 Žnjan, Split
This large pebble beach 4 km (2 miles) east of central Split is well equipped with trampolines and playparks.

7 Bačvice Beach, Split
The sandy bottom of Bačvice Bay is famously shallow, making it perfect for safe paddling and playing.

8 Banje Beach, Dubrovnik
The banana boat rides are popular with older kids in summer (see p48).

9 Klis Fortress
This grizzled medieval fortress (see p88) situated above the village of the same name will fire the imagination.

10 Soko grad Fortress
The dramatic location of this clifftop castle is as stirring as they come; and there's an audiovisual display inside.

🔟 Restaurants

Sashimi at Bugenvila, Cavtat

1 Bugenvila, Cavtat
A beautiful location, smooth service and plenty of imagination in the kitchen make this one of the best places to eat (see p101) in Southern Dalmatia. Only freshly sourced food is served, and the menu changes accordingly. Excellent cocktails, too.

2 Pojoda, Vis Town
A superb seafood restaurant (see p83), Pojoda is famed for serving many of the old island recipes that have been forgotten elsewhere, with barley and chickpeas featuring alongside quality fish and lobster.

3 Vila Koruna, Mali Ston
Dine on oysters and mussels plucked straight from the waters in front of the restaurant (see p101). The food is spiced with *fleur de sel* (flower of salt) from the salt plain in Ston, the oldest active saltworks in the world. The restaurant is equally adept at conjuring up creative dishes with fish and shellfish.

4 Bakus, Ston
Ston is considered the oyster capital of Southern Dalmatia, but Bakus (see p101) serves much more besides, with locally caught fish and home-grown vegetables drawing locals and visiting gourmets alike. The seafood pasta dishes are outstanding, but leave room for a dessert.

5 Speeza, Hvar Town
A gourmet favourite, this new restaurant (see p88) has the owner-chef working in an open kitchen. The chef prepares as well as designs menus on the spot for guests. The tasting menu is recommended, as is booking in advance.

6 Jastožera, Komiža
The fishing port of Komiža is famous for its lobster, and Jastožera (see p83) is the best place to eat it. The name itself means "The Lobster Pen", and the tables are set around a large stone tank in which the freshly caught specimens are kept, before being served in many ways. The fish here is also first class.

7 Noštromo, Split
This is the best place to eat (see p93) in the centre of town. It is just by the fish market, so the seafood is about as fresh as it gets. The decor is light and airy – a refreshing change from nautical theming.

8 Nautika, Dubrovnik
Long the most famous restaurant in the city, Nautika (see p75) has many would-be detractors, but it usually hits the spot for most diners. The menu nods towards the Adriatic with locally sourced

Nautika, Dubrovnik

fish, but there are also meat and vegetarian dishes. Vying for centre stage, though, are the wonderful views of the Old City to one side and Lovrijenac Fortress to the other from the lovely terrace.

9 Adio Mare, Korčula Town

This bustling seafood restaurant (see p83), awarded two toques by Gault & Millau in 2018, is located in the old quarter of Korčula town, close to the reputed birthplace of Marco Polo. Fragrant smoke billows from the fish grill, beckoning in the crowds – but despite the volume of diners, the restaurant manages to maintain great quality, and few leave unsatisfied.

The busy dining area at Adio Mare in Korčula town

10 Orsan, Dubrovnik

Away from the crowds, in Dubrovnik's Old City, local foodies flock here (see p75) for classic Dalmatian seafood dishes and a classic view. The menu includes octopus salad, black risotto (prepared with cuttlefish ink), freshly caught fish and a limited selection of meat dishes. The best places to eat are at the pine-tree-shaded outdoor tables, right by the water's edge, along the quay of the Orsan Yacht Club marina.

TOP 10 CULINARY HIGHLIGHTS

Local scampi – a popular choice

1 Scampi (Buzara)
This rich and flavoursome seafood dish is a Dalmatian speciality. Scampi are gently simmered in a sauce of tomato, onion and herbs.

2 Ston Oysters (Oštrige)
Head to Mali Ston for divine oysters straight from the beds just offshore.

3 Pag Cheese (Paški Sir)
Pag produces a distinctive salted sheep's cheese – the finest cheese in the country.

4 Black Risotto
Squid is a staple of Adriatic cuisine and is cooked in many ways. Squid risotto, blackened by the squid's natural juices, is a Croatian national favourite.

5 Dalmatian Ham (Pršut)
This air-dried smoked ham, often served as a starter with Pag cheese, is arguably even better than the Italian equivalent.

6 Lamb (Janjetina)
Flavoursome lamb from animals that have been fed on fresh herbs.

7 Lobster (Jastog)
Diners can often select their own lobster from the tank, usually served quite simply.

8 Pašticada
Dalmatia's most famous meat dish is this delicious tangy stew of beef in red wine, plums and tomatoes.

9 Istrian Truffles (Tartufi)
From Croatian Istria, both white and black varieties are often a match for French and Italian truffles.

10 Grilled Fresh Fish
Dalmatia's signature dish is disarmingly straightforward: fresh fish, grilled as simply as possible. Salt and olive oil are the only other essentials.

For a key to restaurant price ranges see p75

🔟 **Things to Buy**

1 Chocolate

Locally made chocolates are an increasingly important part of the confectionery scene. A dash of Adriatic character is provided by the use of local flavourings: mandarins, lemons, figs, carob (rogač), lavender and sea salt are among some of the most common additions.

2 Wine

Quality Dalmatian wines include the reds Plavac, Dingač and Postup from the Pelješac Peninsula. Grk and Pošip (white) are grown in Korčula. Vineyards in the Konavle region produce delectable Dubrovačka Malvazija (also white). Outside of Dalmatia, Žlahtina from the island of Krk, Graševina from Slavonia, and Istrian Malvazija – again all white – are also excellent. It's best to buy direct from the vineyard – otherwise, from a Vinoteka (wine shop).

3 Croatian Spirits

Dalmatians are fond of grape-, herb- and fruit-based spirits that come under the general name of rakija and are drunk as aperitifs or digestifs. Lozovača is made from grapes and is rather like Italian grappa. Travarica is the same thing but with the flavoursome addition of local herbs. A number of delicious rakijas are made from local fruits, such as fig (smokva), carob, bilberry

A range of Croatian spirits

(borovnica) and walnut (orahovača). Nicely packaged bottles make excellent souvenirs.

A selection of lace souvenirs

4 Lace

Available in many guises, including tablecloths, handkerchiefs and clothing, lace can be bought in boutiques throughout Dalmatia. If you are looking for something really authentic, buy intricate hand-woven lace made by Pag islanders, or pick up a piece crafted by nuns in Hvar town using the leaves of agave plants, which grow on the island.

5 Ties

You could be forgiven for thinking the word "cravat" is French, but it is actually derived from the Croatian word hrvat, which literally means Croat. During the Thirty Years' War, the French cavalry noticed that Croatians wore their scarves in a distinctive manner – which they termed à la cravate ("Croatian-style"). Quality ties can be bought in branches of the Croata (see p72) store in Dubrovnik and Split.

6 Jewellery

Dalmatia is particularly well known for its red Adriatic corals and jewellery. The quality and price of goods depend on the vendor. Upmarket boutiques in Hvar town and on the island of Zlarin are reliable for contemporary coral pieces. Jewellers in Zadar and Dubrovnik are good for silver and gold.

7 Lavender

This fragrant plant has been cultivated on Hvar for the past 75 years, and the myriad oils and balms produced provide an important source of revenue for the islanders. In late spring and early summer, the scent of lavender pervades the island, and a host of products are sold at stalls around Hvar town.

8 Food

Paški sir (Pag cheese), *pršut* (air-dried smoked ham), olive oil and honey are all first-rate food products. If you can, buy direct from locals (look out for the handmade signs displayed on the roadside), or from fresh-food markets. Failing that, you will also find these items in supermarkets and tourist shops.

Croatian cured meats

9 Dolls in Traditional Costume

Dolls in traditional dress are ubiquitous throughout Dalmatia. There are dozens of varieties, from cheap and cheerful souvenirs to more expensive figures wearing handmade clothes. Ceramic dolls are a more contemporary version.

10 Local Designers

A design boom in Croatia has seen a flurry of local creatives putting their ideas into production. Highly individual bags, brooches, scarves and couture can be picked up in Split and Hvar town. Domestic items are also worth looking out for.

TOP 10 TIPS FOR BUYING ART AND CRAFTS

Delicatessen goods from Uje

1 Uje, Dubrovnik
Quality olive oil is the focus here, but there are also *rakija*, biscuits and soaps *(see p72)*. There are also branches in Bol, Korčula, Split, Trogir and Vis.

2 Dubrovačka Kuća, Dubrovnik
This is a quality gift shop and art gallery *(see p72)*.

3 Delicium Nostrum, Trogir
MAP B3 ▪ Obrov 2
The perfect place to buy local delicacies and Croatian wines.

4 Sebastian, Dubrovnik
MAP G9 ▪ Svetog Dominika 5
Interesting gallery selling work by famous artists from former Yugoslavia.

5 Prokurative, Split
MAP L2 ▪ Trg Republike
Clothes and accessory designers sell at this open-air weekend market.

6 Hvaroom, Hvar Town
MAP C4 ▪ Trg svetog Stjepana
Find quality accessories, prints and postcards at this friendly boutique.

7 Diocletian's Palace, Split
The souvenir stalls in the main hall stock a wide selection of art *(see p30)*.

8 Bonbonnière Kraš, Dubrovnik
MAP G9 ▪ Zamanjina 2
This famous Croatian producer of quality chocolates sells pralines, biscuits, cookies and liquors.

9 Life According to KAWA, Dubrovnik
MAP H8 ▪ Hvarska 2
This one-stop souvenir and design store is great for cosmetics and wines.

10 Nadalina, Split
MAP N2 ▪ Dioklecijanova 6
Nadalina's unique chocolate bars make highly desirable souvenirs.

🔟 Dubrovnik and the Dalmatian Coast for Free

1 Watching Sunsets from the Porporela, Dubrovnik

Dubrovnik is blessed with spectacular Adriatic sunsets, and there are few better places to watch them than the Porporela, the man-made breakwater that stretches eastwards from the Old City. You can reach it by taking the coastal path from the old port.

Glorious views from the Serpentina

2 Going to the Beach, Dubrovnik

You may have to pay to use a parasol and a sun lounger, but Dubrovnik's beaches are free to all. Just be sure to position your towel on an available space away from the beach bars. Note, however, that in Croatia you can't reserve a space – towels left out overnight will be confiscated.

3 Coastal Strolls, Dubrovnik

There are any number of seaside promenades on offer outside Dubrovnik's Old City. For a truly scenic walk, take the path that leads from Lapad Beach around the Babin Kuk peninsula, passing coastal rock formations on the way.

4 Scaling Mount Srđ via the Serpentina

Ascending the ridge above Dubrovnik by cable car can be exhilarating, but nothing beats conquering the peak yourself. A zigzagging path called the Serpentina will get you there from the Old City in about 80 minutes. The walk is unshaded, so remember to take water and a hat.

5 Strolling the Old City Streets of Dubrovnik

In many ways, Dubrovnik's greatest tourist attraction is the Old City itself. Exploring the piazzas and palazzos of this compact but eternally fascinating area will tell you more about the city's history than any museum visit.

6 Exploring Diocletian's Palace, Split

It's rare to find a spectacular historical site that can be entered for free, but this is what you get in Diocletian's Palace, which has been adapted over the centuries to form the heart of modern Split. Since it is filled with bars, shops, dwellings and churches, it can't be fenced and an entrance fee charged.

Diocletian's Palace in Split

7 Wandering the Biokovo Botanical Garden

Paths above the resort of Makarska lead up onto the lower slopes of the Biokovo range, the site of a unique botanical garden devoted to highland plants. It is a good introduction to the local flora, and there are also great views of the coast.

8 Relaxing in Đorđić-Mayneri Park, Lopud

Right on the seafront in Lopud, the Đorđić-Mayneri Park is one of the few 19th-century gardens in Dalmatia that has been restored to something approaching its former glory. It is rich in trees, with palm varieties from around the world.

Đorđić-Mayneri Park, Lopud

9 Enjoying the View from Marjan Hill, Split

Marjan, the hilly peninsula that stretches west of central Split, is a huge wooded park that provides the city with its main recreation zone. You can scale the central summit of Telegrin, or walk around the south side to enjoy expansive Adriatic views.

10 Enjoying Street Festivals

Annual feast days and festivals (see pp62–3) can fill the streets with revellers until the early morning, providing an extrovert urban buzz that is open to all. The big dates are the Feast of St Blaise in Dubrovnik (3 February) and the Feast of St Domnius (7 May) in Split. During the tourist season, events such as the Makarska Cultural Summer (June–August) provide outdoor concerts and a street-party atmosphere.

TOP 10 BUDGET TIPS

Scenic foot-passenger ferry

1 Ferry by Foot
Don't take a car on a ferry to the islands unless you really have to. It's cheaper to travel as a foot passenger and hire a car when

2 Stay in an Apartment
A self-catering apartment will usually be cheaper than a hotel room for the same number of people.

3 Visit Independent Cafés
Grab your morning coffee outside the Old City in a bar used by locals. It will be cheaper – and probably better, too.

4 Eat at Small Restaurants
Look for restaurants with daily specials or set lunches listed on a board outside.

5 Off-Peak Trips
Accommodation prices are at their height from June to September. Travel out of season for money-saving deals.

6 Buy a Big Parasol
Invest in your own beach parasol or tent in order to avoid the high daily rental costs.

7 Drink Local
Sample the excellent local wines instead of choosing the more expensive imported varieties.

8 Scenic Slow Boats
Take the slow boat to the islands by travelling with ferries rather than the faster but more expensive catamarans.

9 Make Your Own Meals
Skip restaurants altogether by stocking up on delicious local cheeses, hams and fruits at local markets.

10 Buy Return Tickets
If you are travelling along the coast by bus, purchasing a return ticket will be cheaper than buying two singles.

📋**10** Festivals and Events

① Feast of St Blaise, Dubrovnik

On 3 February, Dubrovnik's citizens mark the life and work of their patron saint and protector *(see p45)*. The celebrations begin at 10am, with a Mass outside the cathedral. At 11:30am, reliquaries of St Blaise are carried around the city.

② Carnival

Spectacular Shrove Tuesday processions are held in Split, where masked locals burn an effigy of Krnje, a mythical figure that represents all the ills that have befallen the city over the previous year. On the same day, in a celebration known as Poklad, the inhabitants of Lastovo commemorate a 15th-century victory of the islanders over pirates; a puppet is chased, captured and burned at the stake.

③ Feast of St Domnius, Split

Split's patron saint is celebrated on 7 May, with locals lining the Riva to watch the religious procession before heading to the Palace area. Stalls on the Riva sell souvenirs of the day.

④ Mediterranean Film Festival, Split

Early Jun ▪ www.fmfs.hr

This week-long festival showcases new films with a Southern European focus. Screenings take place at the Zlatna Vrata cinema in the Palace district and at the outdoor cinema on the beach at Bačvice.

⑤ Concert Season at Orsula Park, Dubrovnik

A hillside park just outside Dubrovnik makes an enchanting venue for a summer-long season of concerts featuring the best rock, jazz and world-music acts from Croatia and the surrounding region. With lovely views of the Old City down below, it's a stirring spot to spend an evening.

⑥ Split Summer Festival

Mid-Jul–late Aug ▪ www. splitsko-ljeto.hr

Opera, ballet, classical music, pop, and a diverse array of theatrical performances heighten the energy in Dalmatia's largest city. Open-air productions held in Diocletian's Palace *(see pp30–31)* are the highlight, with the staging of Verdi's *Aida* in the Peristyle an enduring favourite.

⑦ Dubrovnik Festival

Mid-Jul–late Aug
▪ www.dubrovnik-festival.hr

For several decades, stages in historic venues, churches and the open air have filled the Old City with theatre, dance and music. Performances of Shakespeare in the Lovrijenac Fortress tend to sell out quickly.

Performers at the Dubrovnik Festival

8 Moreška, Korčula Town

This traditional 15th-century sword-dance *(see p26)*, staged in Korčula town on the Feast of St Theodore (29 July) and on Mondays and Thursdays in high season, portrays good and evil kings fighting for the affections of a beautiful maiden. This war dance is accompanied with music from a brass band.

The Moreška sword-dance

9 Days of Diocletian, Split

Split's most famous resident is celebrated over a few days in late August, with a local actor playing the role of the Emperor to lead suitably costumed revellers. Cafés fill up, and the narrow streets are transformed into one big outdoor party and the sounds of drums and music can be heard in all the alleys of the city.

10 Summer Festivals

In July and August, summer festivals lasting anything from 2 weeks to 2 months fill the cultural calendars of many towns throughout Dalmatia, with dance, theatre and music gracing outdoor and indoor stages. Some of the liveliest festivals are held in Cavtat, Hvar town, Makarska, Ston and Trogir.

TOP 10 VENUES

Poljud Stadium, Split

1 Poljud Stadium, Split
Home to Hajduk Split football team, the Poljud also hosts rock concerts and the Ultra festival of techno music.

2 Rector's Palace, Dubrovnik
Classical concerts are staged in the open-air atrium *(see pp18–19)* from April to October.

3 Sponza Palace, Dubrovnik
Atmospheric venue in the inner courtyard of this 16th-century palace *(see p14)*.

4 Church of St Saviour, Dubrovnik
This Renaissance church *(see p15)* in the Old City hosts classical concerts every Monday at 9pm.

5 Town Theatre, Hvar Town
Trg Svetog Stjepana ▪ 021 742 935
One of Europe's earliest theatres.

6 Open-Air Theatre, Korčula Town
This compact circular arena overlooks the harbour and offers stunning views of the Pelješac Peninsula.

7 Orsula Park, Dubrovnik
This unique outdoor venue in a natural amphitheatre overlooks a medieval chapel and the Adriatic coast.

8 Open-Air Cinema, Vis Town
Of all Croatia's summer cinemas, this is the most charming, situated right by the sea on Vis town's beautiful bay.

9 Croatian National Theatre, Split
Trg Gaje Bulata 1 ▪ 021 344 999
Impressive theatre hosting opera, ballet and classical music performances.

10 Marin Držić Theatre, Dubrovnik
Pred Dvorom 3 ▪ 020 321 088
Ornate venue staging a wide-ranging theatrical programme.

Dubrovnik and the Dalmatian Coast Area by Area

Boats moored at the pretty waterfront in Komiža, on the island of Vis

🔟 Dubrovnik

Byron called it "The Pearl of the Adriatic". George Bernard Shaw suggested it was "paradise on earth". Now fully recovered from the Serbian and Montenegrin siege of 1991–2, this remarkable former city-state has perhaps the most attractive and well-preserved Baroque core of any European city, its swathe of churches, palaces and old stone houses contained within the sturdy walls that have protected its famed *libertas* (freedom) for centuries. Much of what you see today is the result of painstaking reconstruction after the 1667 earthquake; now, new building work is strictly controlled, even down to the shade of green to be used on the shutters of the city's main thoroughfare, the Stradun.

Column from the Rector's Palace

① Cathedral
MAP G10 ▪ Poljana Marina Držića ▪ 020 323 459 ▪ Treasury: open Apr–Oct: 9am–5pm Mon–Sat, 11am–5pm Sun; Nov–Mar: 10am–noon & 3–5pm Mon–Sat, 11am–noon & 3–5pm Sun ▪ Adm

Erected after the 1667 earthquake, today's Baroque cathedral (see p45), crafted by Italian architects, replaced an earlier Romanesque structure. It houses more than 200 reliquaries,

View over Dubrovnik's Old City

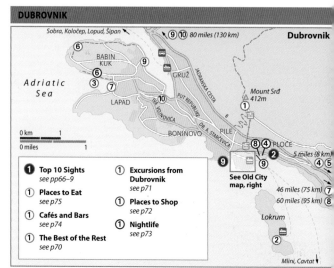

DUBROVNIK

Sobra, Koločep, Lopud, Šipan ➔ ⑨⑩ 80 miles (130 km)   **Dubrovnik**

Adriatic Sea

BABIN KUK

GRUŽ

LAPAD

BONINOVO

Mount Srđ 412m

PILE

PLOČE

5 miles (8 km)

0 km   1
0 miles   1

Lokrum

46 miles (75 km) ⑦
60 miles (95 km) ⑧

Mlini, Cavtat ↓

① **Top 10 Sights** *see pp66–9*	① **Excursions from Dubrovnik** *see p71*
① **Places to Eat** *see p75*	① **Places to Shop** *see p72*
① **Cafés and Bars** *see p74*	① **Nightlife** *see p73*
① **The Best of the Rest** *see p70*	

See Old City map, right

including a 12th-century Byzantine case containing the skull of St Blaise, and casks containing his hands and one leg. It also has what is claimed to be a fragment of the cross on which Jesus was crucified, and a copy of Raphael's *Virgin of the Chair*, reputedly made by the grand master himself.

② Museum of Modern Art, Dubrovnik

MAP K9 ■ Put Frana Supila 23 ■ 020 426 590 ■ Open 9am–8pm Tue–Sun ■ Adm ■ www.momad.hr

Housed in a Neo-Renaissance-cum-Gothic-style villa in affluent Ploče, this museum is the perfect setting for an eclectic array of exhibitions. Look out for sculptures by Ivan Meštrović (1883–1962) *(see p46)* and portraits by Vlaho Bukovac (1855–1922).

③ Dominican Monastery

MAP G8 ■ Svetog Dominika 4 ■ 020 322 200 ■ Open May–Oct: 9am–6pm daily; Nov–Apr: 9am–5pm daily ■ Adm ■ www.dominicanmuseum.hr

The Dominicans were allowed into the city in the 14th century as long as they helped to protect its eastern entrance. The building of the monastery began in 1315, but it was later rebuilt. The

The Dominican monastery and port

monastery buildings of today – the church and library – were built from scratch after almost complete destruction by the 1667 earthquake. Highlights include the Gothic cloisters, 14th-century Italian painter Paolo Veneziano's *Crucifixion* (in the church), and the museum, which houses Titian's *St Blaise, St Mary Magdalene, the Angel Tobias and the Purchaser* – the man on his knees is a member of the then-powerful Gučetić (Gozze) family, who funded the work.

④ Rector's Palace

The post of Rector of Dubrovnik was the ultimate job-share; each incumbent held it for just one month. For that brief period, this was his home *(see pp18–19)*.

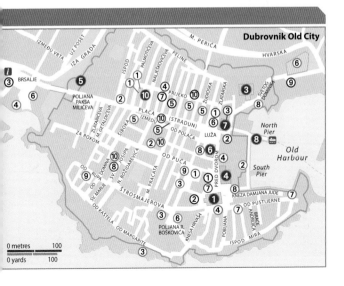

Dubrovnik Old City

0 metres 100
0 yards 100

5 City Walls

There are few better ways to begin your exploration of Dubrovnik than a walk around the city walls *(see pp12–13)*.

6 Church of St Blaise

The original 14th-century church survived the 1667 earthquake *(see p15)* largely intact, only to burn down in a fire in 1706. Work started on the present incarnation later the same year, to plans by Italian architect Marino Gropelli, who based the design of the interior on that of a Baroque church in his home town. Punctuating the ornate façade are four pillars watched over by an array of saints *(see p45)*. The stained-glass windows are also striking – a late-20th-century addition of an unusual kind in this part of Europe.

Stone mask on a fountain in the Old City

7 Stradun and Sponza Palace

The main artery of the Old City is the Stradun *(see pp14–15)*, a stone-paved strip that runs past a stately row of houses that was built after the earthquake of 1667. One of the few buildings that survived the quake was Paskoje Miličević's Sponza Palace (1506–22) at the eastern end of the Stradun. Boasting Renaissance arcades and Venetian-Gothic windows, it is now home to the city archives.

8 Old Harbour
MAP H9

Dubrovnik's first harbour stood to the west side of the city, between the Pile Gate and the Lovrijenac Fortress, but it failed to offer sufficient shelter, and in any case soon became too small as the city grew. The Old Harbour, on the east side of the Old City, is a much grander affair, with the Revelin and St John's forts guarding either flank. Amenities are limited here, but there are one or two places to eat, and take in the busy summer scene; there's always a flurry of small fishing boats and tourist craft enjoying the harbour's protection, and there are good views down the coast towards Cavtat.

A sunny panorama across Dubrovnik Old Harbour

The imposing Lovrijenac Fortress

9 Lovrijenac Fortress

MAP J9 ▪ 020 324 641
▪ Open 9am–6pm daily ▪ Adm

This sweeping fortress rises steeply out of the Adriatic to the west of the city walls. Historically it served both as a place to store the city's gold and a military hub and battery where the city could be brought to heel in the event of a rebellion. The city's slogan guards the entrance: "Freedom must not be sold for all the gold in the world." The fortress is one of the most atmospheric venues of the Dubrovnik Festival (see pp62–3), with Shakespeare soliloquies echoing across the old ramparts. It's a tough climb on a hot day, but well worth it.

10 War Photo Limited

MAP F9 ▪ Antuninska 6
▪ 020 322 166 ▪ Open May–Sep: 10am–10pm daily; Apr & Oct: 10am–4pm Mon & Wed–Sun
▪ www.warphotoltd.com ▪ Adm

Just off the Stradun, this exhibition centre displays works by the world's top war and conflict photographers. Under the curation of New Zealander Wade Goddard, himself a former war photographer, the centre exposes the horrors and ugliness of war that are all too often sanitized by the media. Its changing exhibitions are thought-provoking, informative and often heartbreaking. The centre itself, set over two floors, is a well-planned space that shows the photographs as traditional framed prints or as digital presentations. One room holds a permanent display of images and multimedia from the conflicts that tore Yugoslavia apart in the 1990s.

A DAY IN DUBROVNIK

▶ MORNING

If you're an early riser, climb the **City Walls** when they open (9am) and you may have them largely to yourself. Make a leisurely circuit taking in their sights (see pp12–13) and watching the city as it gradually comes to life below. Stop at **St John's Fort** (see p13) to visit the **Maritime Museum** (see pp46–7) and **Aquarium** (see p70). Descend to the **Stradun** (see pp14–15), and if you didn't take breakfast at your hotel, enjoy a coffee and a pastry at the **Festival Café** (see p74) – it's a great vantage-point from which to observe the frenetic street life of the city's main artery.

Continue strolling gently down the Stradun, just absorbing the atmosphere rather than delving into its various attractions. Enjoy an early seafood lunch at noon in **Kamenice** (see p75), and absorb the colourful sights and sounds of the market in **Gundulićeva Poljana** (see p70).

AFTERNOON

After lunch, head across to the **Rector's Palace** (see pp18–19) and take a self-guided audio tour. Continue around to the start of the Stradun at Luža Square. From here you can choose which of this pedestrianized area's attractions to explore (see pp14–15) as you travel its length towards the **Pile Gate** (see p12) and a warm welcome at the **Café Dubravka** (see p74), or perhaps take an early dinner at **Nautika** (see p75), and enjoy glorious views over one of Europe's most stunning cities.

See map on pp66–7 ⬅

The Best of the Rest

Statue in Gundulićeva Poljana

1 Gundulićeva Poljana (Gundulić Square)
MAP G9

This beautiful square is home to a statue of Ivan Gundulić, the 17th-century poet whose *Osman* recalls a great Slavic victory over the Turks. There's a lively morning market here.

2 Orthodox Church Museum
MAP F9 ■ Od Puča 8 ■ 020 323 283 ■ Currently closed for restoration ■ Adm

Two doors down from the refurbished Serbian Orthodox Church (see p45) is this colourful Icon Museum with works dating from the 15th to 19th centuries.

3 Church of St Ignatius
MAP F10 ■ Poljana R Boškovića ■ Open 8am–7pm daily

Up a grand sweep of stairs, modelled on Rome's Spanish Steps, is this voluminous 18th-century Jesuit Church. Its dim interior houses fine examples of trompe l'oeil.

4 Pustijerna
MAP G10

Wander the streets of this area to the south of the Stradun in search of traces of the city walls. Medieval houses, many in ruins, huddle along impossibly narrow lanes, giving an insight into pre-1667 Dubrovnik.

5 Synagogue
MAP G9 ■ Žudioska 5 ■ Open daily (Nov–Apr: Mon–Fri) ■ Adm

This little synagogue, up the hill from the Stradun, is said to be Europe's second oldest, after one in Prague.

6 Archaeology Collection
MAP H8 ■ Revelin Fort ■ 020 324 041 ■ Open 10am–4pm Thu–Tue ■ Adm

This small exhibition is on the lower storeys of the 16th-century Revelin Fort. Many of the stone carvings once adorned the city's churches.

7 Aquarium
MAP H10 ■ Fort of St John ■ 020 323 978 ■ Open May & Oct: 9am–8pm daily; Jun–Sep: 9am–9pm daily; Nov–Apr: 9am–4pm daily ■ Adm

The Aquarium is a good rainy-day choice, with its poisonous Adriatic moray eels, stingrays and seahorses.

8 Dulčić-Masle-Pulitika Gallery
MAP G10 ■ Držićeva poljana 1 ■ 020 323 172 ■ Open 9am–8pm Tue–Sun ■ Adm

Dubrovnik was home to a generation of Expressionist painters. Work by Ivo Dulčić (1916–75), Antun Masle (1919–67) and Đuro Pulitika (1922–2006) is on display here.

9 Rupe Ethnographic Museum
MAP F9 ■ Od Rupa 3 ■ 020 323 018 ■ Open 9am–4pm, Mon, Wed–Sun (Apr–mid-Oct: until 6pm) ■ Adm

This vast space was built to store grain, in holes bored into the rock, in case of siege. The museum looks at daily life over the years.

10 House of Marin Držić
MAP F9 ■ Široka 7 ■ Open Jun–Sep: 10am–6pm Mon, 9am–8:30pm Tue–Sun; Oct–May: 9am–8:30pm Tue–Sun ■ Adm

This museum honours a celebrated 16th-century Dubrovnik playwright.

See map on pp66–7

Excursions from Dubrovnik

1 Mount Srđ
MAP K8

Modern cable cars ascend Mount Srd in fewer than four minutes for amazing views. The Napoleonic fortress at the summit holds a museum devoted to the 1991–2 siege.

2 Lokrum

Temptingly positioned just offshore is an unspoiled island (see pp20–21) that is a world away from the city, with quiet coves, an old monastery and a crumbling fort. Boats leave from the old port.

3 Lapad Bay
MAP H8

Squeezed between the Lapad and Babin Kuk peninsulas, this broad shallow bay is home to one of Dubrovnik's most popular family beaches. The pedestrianized Kralja Zvonimira is abuzz with cafés.

4 Srebreno
MAP H6

Right next to Mlini, Srebreno is an up-and-coming resort, with a plush hotel and shopping mall overlooking its broad sweep of a bay. The shoreline promenade takes you past busy cafés and a children's playpark.

5 Mlini
MAP H6

This small fishing village 11 km (7 miles) south of Dubrovnik has a palm-lined waterfront and traditional stone houses. Numerous streams and a beach add to Mlini's appeal.

6 Babin Kuk Peninsula
MAP J8

Sharing the same rump of land as Lapad, Babin Kuk is another beach-lined peninsula that is a pleasant area for walking and swimming.

7 Kotor
MAP K7

Cross the border into Montenegro, and your reward is the nearest the Adriatic has to a fjord – the stunning Kotor Bay – and the charming historical town of Kotor itself.

8 Sveti Stefan

Further on into Montenegro, this hotel resort on its own island was once a favourite of the international jet set. Today's day-trippers can walk the island and dine in the restaurant.

9 Mostar

The old bridge that gave the city its name has been expertly restored following its notorious destruction during the 1990s conflict. It is the top sight in this city (see p91) in Bosnia-Herzegovina, close to the Croatian border.

10 Međugorje
MAP F4

Even during the war, pilgrims flocked to this spot in Bosnia-Herzegovina, where the Virgin Mary is said to have appeared in 1981. Hordes of visitors have tainted things a bit, but this is still a remarkable place to visit.

Boats in the bay at Mlini

Places to Shop

1 Modni Kantun
MAP G9 ■ Zlatarska 3

Tucked into an alley behind the Sponza Palace, "Fashion Corner" specializes in clothes by Croatian designers, featuring plenty that is practical, stylish and unique. They also stock hats, bags and jewellery.

2 Dubrovačka Kuća (Dubrovnik House)
MAP H9 ■ Svetog Dominika bb

This is a charming gallery-cum-gift shop selling quality Croatian wines, Istrian truffles, traditional souvenirs and original paintings.

3 Vinoteka Miličić
MAP G9 ■ Placa 2

A great little wine shop in the heart of the Old City that sells local and imported alcoholic drinks, alongside olive oil. The entrance is from the Stradun.

4 Medusa
MAP G8 ■ Prijeko 18

Great for souvenir shopping, Medusa stocks Croatian products such as original, handmade Croatian craftwork, wooden toys, natural cosmetics and local food. It also exhibits paintings by local artists.

The entrance to Medusa

5 Algebra
MAP G9 ■ Placa 9

This centrally located bookstore is a great place to browse through a wide range of books including the works of Croatian writers translated into English. It is also a useful shop for visitors wanting to pick up travel guides and souvenirs.

6 Tilda
MAP G9 ■ Zlatarska 1

A tiny souvenir shop tucked between the Stradun and Prijeko, Tilda stocks a range of traditional clothes and hand-woven scarfs, as well as cloth and bags with intricate hand-embroidery.

7 Croata
MAP G9 ■ Pred Dvorom 2

Where better to buy a tie than the country in which they were created? At Croata visitors can shop for ties, scarves and shawls, handmade from the finest silk, with unique designs. There are also branches in Split.

8 Atelijer Ivona's House
MAP F9 ■ Svetog Josipa 12

Around the corner from the Orthodox Church Museum in the Old City, this little store is packed with funky modern handmade jewellery created by Ivona Matica. There is a second store in the capital, Zagreb.

9 Life According to KAWA
MAP H8 ■ Hvarska 2

Housed in a renovated garage above Ploče Gate, this delightful store sells local delicacies, craft beer, wine, coffee and clothes designed by local designers and artisans.

10 Uje
MAP G9 ■ Placa bb

Uje is one of the main outlets for quality Croatian olive oil, notably their own-brand Bracchia, a smooth aromatic oil from the island of Brač. It also sells a range of preserves, local capers, and chocolates.

Nightlife

1 Nonenina
MAP G9 ■ Pred Dvorom 4

This centrally located bar has outdoor tables and comfy seating looking out onto the Rector's Palace, making it a perfect spot for evening cocktails.

2 Troubadour Hard Jazz Café
MAP G10 ■ Bunićeva Poljana

Tables at this vibrant bolthole pour out onto the square behind the cathedral. Regular live music performances keep the place constantly busy. Don't worry if you can't get a seat, as the music can be heard from the neighbouring bars too.

3 Sky Bar
MAP E8 ■ Brsalje 8

Formerly known as Fuego, cult disco Sky Bar packs in locals and visitors with its eclectic mix of dance music (from pop hits to niche techno styles) and live acts. A well-stocked bar and a great location just outside Pile Gate help ensure its enduring popularity.

4 Banje Beach Club
MAP H8 ■ Frana Supila bb

On Banje beach, this chic club is the place to party come sunset, with magical views of the floodlit city walls across the water.

5 B4 Revelin
MAP G9 ■ Vetranićeva 3

A pre-club bar run by the same people as Culture Club Revelin, B4 mixes a hip dance soundtrack and an array of cocktails and shots. This popular spot is frequently standing room only.

6 Cave Bar More
MAP J8 ■ Nika i Meda Pucića 13

Situated in a natural cave, this bar has outdoor tables overlooking Lapad Bay. It is a beautiful spot to have great cocktails or just a glass of local beer while enjoying the sunset.

7 The Bar by Azur
MAP G8 ■ Kunićeva 5

Popular with locals, this fine bar spread over two levels offers excellent cocktails. There's also a good range of craft brews, gins and Croatian wines.

Contemporary venue Club Lazareti

8 Club Lazareti
MAP H8 ■ Frana Supila 8

An old quarantine house and artisans' workshops now form a venue for alternative, contemporary musical, and theatrical performances and a nightclub with guest DJs. Keep your eyes open for posters, or check with the tourist office to know what's on.

9 Culture Club Revelin
MAP H9 ■ Svetog Dominika 3

Every night the Revelin fort becomes the centre of Dubrovnik's nightlife scene, showcasing electronic music with impressive visuals and lasers.

10 Exit Rock Café
MAP G9 ■ Boškovićeva 4

A long-standing favourite with the locals, this upstairs bar just off the Stradun is considered one of the city's better choices for Croatian craft beer. Expect a cocktail of hard-rock sounds and frequent live bands.

See map on pp66–7

Cafés and Bars

Cosy interior of D'Vino Wine Bar

1 D'Vino Wine Bar
MAP F9 ■ Palmotićeva 4a

This friendly little wine bar, in the heart of the Old City, serves quality Dalmatian wine by the glass or bottle. It is a cosy place with exposed stone walls and subtle lighting.

2 Festival Café
MAP F9 ■ Placa bb

At the western end of the Stradun, this café has a mellow and sophisticated air. Director's chairs on the pavement are great for watching the world go by. If you've been hankering after single-malt Scotch whisky, look no further.

3 Buža
MAP F10 ■ off Od Margarite

On a sunny day follow the signs from Gundulićeva Poljana *(see p70)* to this great open-air bar. Located on the rocks outside the southern walls of the Old City, it has great views over the sea to Lokrum.

4 Gradska Kavana
MAP G9 ■ Pred Dvorom 1

This revamped city café has a terrace that is in the perfect place for a spot of people watching.

5 Katie O'Connor's
MAP G9 ■ Dropčeva 4a

A charming Irish pub is situated in an old stone cellar. Come here for the largest selection of beers, stouts, ales, ciders and spirits in Dubrovnik. The traditional English breakfasts are also a popular draw.

6 Café Dubravka 1836
MAP E8 ■ Brsalje 3

The views from this low-key café's terrace are spectacular. It is located between the Pile Gate and the Lovrijenac Fortress.

7 Lapad Beach
MAP J8 ■ Lapad Bay

This complex on the beach at Lapad Bay combines a restaurant, bar and lounge terrace. It's great for drinks and snacks by day, and, once the sun goes down, a party vibe takes over.

8 La Bodega
MAP G9 ■ Lučarica 1

At the eastern end of the Stradun is La Bodega, which occupies the ground floor and three storeys of a historic house. A different experience is offered on each, from café to wine and tapas bar to party space.

9 Razonoda Wine Bar
MAP G9 ■ Od Puča 1

Sip delectable Croatian and international vintages in the Pucić Palace's elegant wine bar. To accompany the wine there is a menu of Croatian-style tapas, which feature classic cheeses and prosciutto.

10 The Gaffe Pub
MAP G9 ■ Miha Pracata 4

The Gaffe Pub is a more refined version of the Irish theme bar across the street, with a green and dark-wood decor. The staff are friendly, and the atmosphere is relaxed.

The Irish-themed Gaffe Pub

Places to Eat

PRICE CATEGORIES

For a three-course meal for one with half a bottle of wine (or equivalent meal), taxes and extra charges.

K under 150kn   KK 150–250kn
KKK over 250kn

1 Nishta
MAP F8 ▪ Prijeko bb ▪ 020 322 088 ▪ Closed Jan–Feb ▪ KK

Dubrovnik's only vegan restaurant has a superb salad bar and offers miso and gazpacho soups. Book ahead in summer.

2 Lokanda Peskarija
MAP H10 ▪ Na Ponti bb ▪ 020 324 750 ▪ Closed 25 Dec–1 Feb ▪ K

Lokanda Peskarija serves a simple menu of mussels, squid, seafood risotto and scampi. Outdoor benches overlook the Old Harbour, and the rustic interior is atmospheric.

3 Kamenice
MAP G10 ▪ Gundulićeva Poljana 8 ▪ 020 323 682 ▪ K

Gorge on huge plates of fried squid, fresh mussels, seafood risotto and grilled scampi, washed down with a crisp house white. It's great value, and the outdoor setting is wonderful.

4 Nautika
MAP E9 ▪ Brsalje 1 ▪ 020 442 526 ▪ Closed Dec–Jan ▪ KKK

Share an Adriatic fish platter or Chateaubriand with a loved one as the Adriatic laps at the rocks below *(see pp56–7)*.

5 Fish Restaurant Proto
MAP F9 ▪ Široka 1 ▪ 020 323 234 ▪ KKK

Proto shines out above most of the Old City eateries, with a menu that focuses on seafood but also caters to meat-eaters. The terrace on the first floor is the place to be in summer.

6 Kopun
MAP G10 ▪ Boškovićeva poljana 7 ▪ 020 323 969 ▪ Closed Jan ▪ KK

The charmingly situated Kopun is one of the best places for traditional specialities, such as the roast capon that gives this restaurant its name.

Oyster & Sushi Bar Bota

7 Oyster & Sushi Bar Bota
MAP G10 ▪ Od pustijerne bb ▪ 020 324 034 ▪ Closed Oct–Apr ▪ KK

This chic, romantic spot serves some of the best Croatian-Asian fusion food in the Adriatic – think oysters, sushi and tempura.

8 360°
MAP H9 ▪ Sv Dominika bb ▪ 020 322 222 ▪ Closed Mon & Nov–Mar ▪ KKK

A Mediterranean fine-dining menu and huge international wine list are offered in an elegant setting with stunning views of the port.

9 Orsan
MAP J8 ▪ Ivana Zajca 2 ▪ 020 436 822 ▪ Closed Dec ▪ KKK

Serving classic Dalmatian dishes in a seaside setting, Orsan is popular with locals and tourists alike.

10 Otto
MAP J8 ▪ Nikole Tesle 8 ▪ 020 358 633 ▪ Closed Dec ▪ KK

Sited in the former boathouse of an aristocratic mansion, Otto serves seafood and Modern European fare.

See map on pp66–7

🔟 The Dalmatian Islands

Many of Dalmatia's most spectacular features are at their most concentrated on the islands. Centuries of culture are found in historic towns that blend modern tourist facilities with an intimate, welcoming feel. Island landscapes tend towards the raw and uncommercialized, with olive groves, vineyards and Mediterranean maquis spilling over the dry-stone walls built centuries ago by rock-clearing farmers. The main islands are already established destinations: chic but charming Hvar, beachcomber-friendly Brač, vine-carpeted Korčula and distant, unspoiled Vis, many Croats' favourite Adriatic island. Beach connoisseurs will be delighted by the sheer variety of broad shingle bays and semi-secret coves on offer, and by the remarkably clear sea. While ferries and catamarans from Split provide the main means of transportation, a seaplane service also links some of the main resorts.

Sculpture from Korčula's Cathedral of St Mark

THE DALMATIAN ISLANDS

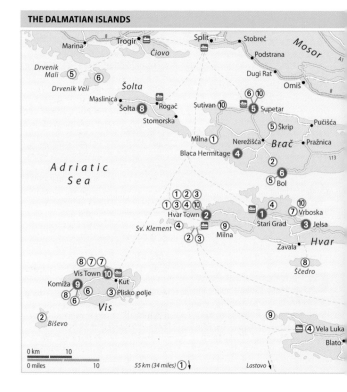

Wooden boats in the harbour at Stari Grad

1 Stari Grad, Hvar
MAP C4 ■ Tourist info: Obala
dr. Franje Tuđmana 1; 021 765 763

Founded by the ancient Greeks,
Stari Grad was for a long time
Hvar's main town. It still serves as
the island's main ferry port, but the
bustle of traffic is kept well away
from the charming centre of
medieval streets, window boxes and
pretty squares. The harbour, with its
ring of stone houses and brand new
yachting marina, makes for a
delightful stroll. Immediately east
of town is the Stari Grad Plain, a
UNESCO-protected patchwork of
fields that has changed little since
ancient Greek times.

2 Hvar Town
MAP C4 ■ Tourist info:
Trg sv Stjepana 42; 021 741 059;
www.tzhvar.hr

Grouped around a horseshoe-shaped
harbour, Hvar town juxtaposes historical town and contemporary tourist
playground. The Riva, with its cocktail
bars and swanky yachts, is a few steps
away from one of the Adriatic's finest
squares, where a cathedral, Venetian
arsenal and Baroque theatre make for
a stunning ensemble. On either side
of the square are former aristocratic
houses that are now restaurants and
specialist shops. There are rocky
bathing spots around the town itself,
and gorgeous sand-and-shingle
beaches on the Pakleni islands, a
short taxi-boat ride across the bay.

3 Jelsa, Hvar
MAP C4 ■ Tourist info: Riva bb;
021 761 017; www.tzjelsa.hr

Jelsa is a relatively unspoiled fishing
port with good beaches. It can be busy
in summer but rarely overpowering.
There is a warren of narrow streets
at its heart and a seaside path to
the village of Vrboska (see p80), 5 km
(3 miles) away. Boats leave for Bol
every morning.

Šestanovac

Zadvarje

Brela

Baška Voda

Sumartin

Podgora

Drvenik

116
Bogomolje

Sućuraj

8

Lovište

Trpanj

414

Korčula

Orebić

Korčula Town

7

118
Smokvica

Lumbarda

Mljet,
Dubrovnik

Brna

5 9 9

7

MARCO POLO

The island of Korčula is alleged by some to be the birthplace of legendary explorer Marco Polo – a claim that has been hotly disputed by both Venice and Genoa. Historians now generally agree that Polo was born in the Venetian Republic, but there is evidence to suggest that he at least visited Korčula Town, so the idea may not be total fantasy. This is something that the locals have seized upon, with "Marco Polo's House" now a museum.

4 Blaca Hermitage, Brač
MAP C4 ▪ 021 637 092
▪ Open 9am–5pm Tue–Sun (mid-Sep–mid-Jun: to 3pm) ▪ Adm

Dramatically situated on the scrub-covered flanks of a ravine, Blaca Hermitage is one of the most-visited former monasteries in Croatia. It was founded in the 16th century by an association of island priests who wanted to establish a monastic community with its own rules. The hermitage can be reached on foot from a car-park a few minutes' uphill walk away.

5 Supetar, Brač
MAP C3 ▪ Tourist info: Porat 1, 021 630 551; www.supetar.hr

An hour away from Split by regular ferry, Supetar is the easiest of the island resorts to reach. It's a charming little spot, grouped around a small-boat harbour and overlooked by a pretty parish church. Supetar's main asset is the broad pebbly bay

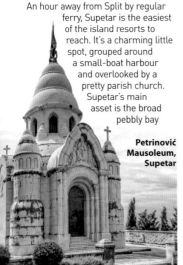

Petrinović Mausoleum, Supetar

just west of the harbour – perfect for a lazy day. Behind the beach looms the spire of the Petrinović Mausoleum, a famously elegant funerary chapel designed by Split-born sculptor Toma Rosandić.

Aerial view of Zlatni Rat, Bol

6 Bol, Brač
MAP C4 ▪ Tourist info: Porat bolskih pomoraca bb; 021 635 638; www.bol.hr

Spreading beneath the vineyard-covered slopes of Vidova Gora, Bol is one of the most popular resorts in Dalmatia on account of its proximity to Zlatni Rat, the magnificent curve of shingle that juts into the sea just west of town. Home to a constant holiday buzz during the summer season, Bol nonetheless has a tranquil Old Town made up of stone houses and narrow streets. Thanks to favourable winds in the channel dividing Brač from Hvar, Bol is a also major centre for windsurfing and kite-surfing, with a string of agencies on the path towards Zlatni Rat renting gear and offering lessons.

7 Korčula Town
The historic core of Korčula town *(see pp26–7)* is one of Dalmatia's most dramatic set-pieces. For the visitor, it offers attractive architecture, fine restaurants and tranquil water-side cafés from which to admire dazzling sunsets. The town is also something of an activity centre, with windsurfing, yachting and diving all popular watersports.

8 Šolta Island
MAP B3 ▪ Tourist info: 021
654 657; www.visitsolta.com

Close to Split but not very touristy, Šolta is the perfect getaway. Covered in maquis, olive trees and dry-stone walls, the island is the ideal place for hiking or cycling. At the western tip of the island, the picturesque port of Maslinica has a small pebble beach and the seaside walk to Šešula Bay, often filled with visiting yachts. The south coast offers beaches and coves, most accessible on foot or by boat.

9 Komiža, Vis
MAP B5 ▪ Tourist info: Riva sv. Mikule 2; 021 713 455; www. tz-komiza.hr

Dramatically situated Komiža spreads around a compact bay surrounded by green slopes. The harbour is backed by narrow alleys, with shingle beaches short stroll away. Komiža is known for its fishing port history. The town has two unique churches in the shape of Our Lady of the Pirates *(see p44)* and the Mušter *(see p45)*.

The pretty town of Komiža

10 Vis Town, Vis
MAP B5 ▪ Tourist info: Šetalište Stare Isse 5; 021 717 017; www.tz-vis.hr

Vis is packed with history: here you'll find Roman baths, a medieval monastery, Austrian-era fortifications and lots of evocative Mediterranean alleys. Highlights include the suburb of Kut, famous for its elegant Renaissance houses, a museum that's bursting with ancient amphorae, and the British-built King George III Fortress 2 km (1 mile) out of town.

A DAY ON BRAČ ISLAND

▶ MORNING

Catch the ferry from Split to **Supetar**, and enjoy the journey from the open upper deck. Take morning coffee on Supetar's delightful harbour before hiring a car or bike from one of the agencies opposite the ferry dock. Ascend south onto the island's central plateau, where a landscape of olive groves, dry-stone enclosures and wild figs provides plenty of photo opportunities. Take a detour to the village of **Škrip** *(see p80)*, site of the absorbing Island of Brač Museum *(see p46)*. Continue south to the resort of **Bol**, taking an early lunch in one of the many good restaurants along the animated Riva.

AFTERNOON

Walk or take the tourist train to the famous beach of **Zlatni Rat** *(see p48)*, west of Bol. Spend the afternoon swimming, kayaking or wake-boarding. If you have kids, let them loose at the aquapark. When the heat begins to recede in late afternoon, drive to the summit of **Vidova Gora** *(see p80)* for glorious views across the Adriatic sea before detouring west to explore the arid and desolate landscape surrounding the **Blaca Hermitage**.

Return to Supetar to drop the car off before taking a seaside stroll to the Petrinović Mausoleum. Enjoy an evening drink at Benny's Bar *(see p82)*, or tuck in to a seafood dinner in Supetar's Bistro Palute *(see p83)*, before catching the last ferry back to Split at 10:45pm.

See map on pp76–7 ←

The Best of the Rest

1 Milna, Brač
MAP C4 ▪ Riva 5
▪ 021 636 233

On the western side of Brač, Milna is a typical Mediterranean fishing village. Now a popular stop-off for yachtspeople, it has a lively marina and some welcoming restaurants.

2 Vidova Gora, Brač
MAP C4

Soaring dramatically above Bol, the grey escarpment of Vidova Gora is, at 778 m (2,552 ft) above sea level, the highest point on any Dalmatian island. It is accessible by car, bike or 3-hour hike for breathtaking views.

3 Plisko Polje, Vis
MAP B5

Most of Vis is rock and scrub, but a green and fertile plain spreads along the southern part of the island, where the village of Plisko Polje is surrounded by vineyards. It's also the site of Dalmatia's only cricket pitch.

4 Vela Luka, Korčula
MAP C5

Korčula town may be the star sight on the island, but don't miss the palm-fringed port of Vela Luka, where Vela Spila cave attests to the presence of prehistoric cultures.

5 Škrip, Brač
MAP C3

Škrip is a well-preserved inland village surrounded by sheep pasture and olive groves. The Island of Brač Museum *(see p46)* has enthralling displays.

6 Mount Hum, Vis
MAP B5

One of the Adriatic's great lookout points, the 587-m (1,926-ft) Mount Hum looms above Komiža on the western side of Vis, offering an expansive panorama.

7 Vrboska, Hvar
MAP C4 ▪ Tourist office: Vrboska bb; 021 774 137

The pretty village of Vrboska is famed for its location on either side of a saltwater channel. The nearby Glavica peninsula is a long rocky beach with naturist-friendly coves.

8 Sućuraj, Hvar
MAP E4 ▪ Tourist office: Riva bb; 021 717 288

Sućuraj's sleepy harbour offers a total contrast to the western Hvar. It's a good choice for beachcombers, with a long stretch of shingle near the centre, and many rocky bays at hand.

9 Milna, Hvar
MAP C4

Just 3 km (2 miles) out of Hvar town, Milna is a largely modern village set in a narrow fold of the island's steep south-facing coast. The Mala Milna shingle beach is a short walk away.

10 Sutivan, Brač
MAP C3 ▪ Tourist office: Trg dr. Franje Tuđmana 1; 021 638 357

The fishing port of Sutivan, just west of Supetar, provides access to long stretches of rocky beach. It's one of Dalmatia's most bicycle-friendly spots, with many marked trails.

Street view of Škrip village, Brač

Smaller Islands

Palagruža with its lighthouse

1 Palagruža (nr Vis)
This rocky slip of land extends out into the Adriatic to the very edge of Croatian waters. The 100-m- (330-ft-) tall lighthouse is the sole structure on the island, which can be reached by private boat.

2 Biševo (nr Vis)
This stunning necklace of unspoiled islands is a paradise for sailors and day-trippers *(see pp22–3)*. For the ultimate escape, head to a deserted island for a taste of "Robinson Crusoe tourism".

3 Jerolim (nr Hvar)
MAP C4

The nearest of the Pakleni islands to Hvar town, Jerolim is celebrated for its anything-goes, naturist-or-clothed beaches. This small island is easily explored on foot.

4 Sveti Kliment (nr Hvar)
MAP B4

The largest and most varied of the Pakleni islands, Sveti Kliment offers a laid-back resort at Palmižana, complete with a beach, restaurants and cactus-filled gardens. Trails lead to quieter areas, with rocky beaches and the occasional rustic restaurant.

5 Drvenik Mali (nr Trogir)
MAP A3

Not actually within the Kornati National Park (as some tour opera-tors say), Drvenik Mali is still a lovely place to spend the day, or to anchor a yacht for an afternoon.

6 Drvenik Veli (nr Trogir)
MAP B3

Connected by a bridge to Ugljan, this island is home to a couple of modest fishing villages and a Benedictine monastery. There are ferry connec-tions to Biograd na Moru.

7 Badija (nr Korčula)
MAP E5

Just off Korčula – and reached by taxi-boat – this small island is home to a community of Franciscan monks. The Franciscan church and monastery are both well preserved and make a striking sight by the sea.

The church and monastery on Badija

8 Šćedro (between Hvar and Korčula)
MAP C5

A safe harbour for sea travellers since ancient times, this small island is now a protected nature park.

9 Proizd (nr Korčula)
A short boat ride from Vela Luka, Proizd *(see p49)* is famous for a trio of beaches that consist of shelving slabs of rock. By evening, the rocks turn orange and pink with the sunset.

10 Zečevo (nr Vrboska, Hvar)
MAP C4

Popular with yachtspeople and day-trippers, Zečevo ("Bunny Island") gets its name from the wild rabbits living in its dense shrubbery. Pristine seas and rock beaches attract predominantly naturist bathers.

See map on pp76–7 ←

Cafés, Bars and Nightlife

The Hula beach bar, Hvar town

① Hula Hula, Hvar Town
MAP C4

This wooden, beachside bar on the coastal path, 15 minutes' walk west of the town, is much loved for its delicious cocktails, ambient music and the amazing sunset views.

② Carpe Diem Beach, Pakleni Islands
MAP C4 ■ Stipanska uvala

Five minutes by boat from Hvar town, this luxurious restaurant turns into a party venue by night, with an impressive DJ line-up.

③ Nonica, Hvar Town
MAP C4 ■ Kroz Burak 23

Those with a passion for cakes should head straight for Nonica ("Granny"), a smart little café that offers wonderful cheesecakes, brownies and biscuits. Nonica's almond-flavoured *Hvorski koloč* is something of a local delicacy.

④ Tri Pršuta, Hvar Town
MAP C4 ■ Petra Hektorovića 5

A selection of Croatian wines, cheese, *pršut* (smoked ham) and *kulen* (spiced salami), old and new furnishings, and a mellow mood combine to make this a convivial spot. The alleyway location, with a scattering of outdoor chairs, provides extra charm.

⑤ Varadero, Bol
MAP C4 ■ Frane Radića 1

In the centre of Bol, on the island of Brač, is this immensely popular summer bar. Cocktails are served to clientele lounging on comfy wicker sofas under straw umbrellas overlooking the harbour. There are live DJ sets most nights.

⑥ Benny's Bar, Supetar
MAP C3 ■ Put Vele Luke bb

At one end of Supetar's beach, Benny's is at the heart of pretty much everything in town, serving the beach bar crowd during the day, and offering cocktails and DJs at night.

⑦ Paradajz Lost, Vis Town
MAP B5 ■ Pod Kulom 5

A small stone square just off the seafront is the location for this alfresco bar with a wide selection of local wines and *rakijas*. The second-hand furniture adds retro chic.

⑧ Fabrika, Komiža, Vis
MAP B5 ■ Riva svetog Mikule 12

Fabrika somehow succeeds at combining a lazy lounge-bar vibe with the buzz of a local pub, serving local wines, *rakijas* and a small menu of burgers and light meals.

⑨ Massimo, Korčula Town
MAP E5 ■ Šetalište Petra Kanavelića bb

Atop one of the town's defensive bastions, this popular summer bar has a unique pulley system for drinks. Appreciate the sunset as the swallows swirl on the skyline.

⑩ Red Baron, Hvar Town
MAP C4 ■ Riva bb

You couldn't wish for a better location on Hvar town's Riva, perfect to watch the catamaran dock or drool over the luxury yachts nearby. With a good choice of shooters, cocktails and spirits, this is one of the island's better-stocked bars.

Places to Eat

PRICE CATEGORIES

For a three-course meal for one with half a bottle of wine (or equivalent meal), taxes and extra charges.

K under 150kn   **KK** 150–250kn
KKK over 250kn

(1) Macondo, Hvar Town
MAP C4 ▪ Marije Maričić 7
▪ 021 742 850 ▪ Closed Nov–Apr ▪ KK

This fairly pricey, top-quality seafood restaurant in Hvar's Old Town is no longer a local secret, so book ahead. In summer you can eat outside.

(2) Speeza, Hvar Town
MAP C4 ▪ Vicka Butorovića 64 ▪
098 917 7386 ▪ Closed Nov–Mar ▪ KKK

Near the town centre, this family-run restaurant has a uniquely designed menu that changes almost daily. Interactive cooking classes can also be booked in advance.

Chic interior of Giaxa, Hvar town

(3) Giaxa, Hvar Town
MAP C4 ▪ Petra Hektorovića 11
▪ 021 741 073 ▪ KK

Fine dining in a Renaissance former palace, with local fish and seafood given a modern European treatment. The desserts are outstanding and the wine list as good as any in town.

(4) Antika, Stari Grad
MAP C4 ▪ Donja kola
▪ 021 765 479 ▪ KK

Just inland from Stari Grad's seafront, Antika serves traditional seafood with panache in a dining room full of knick-knacks and curios. There's an outdoor terrace in the flowery piazza around the corner.

(5) Adio Mare, Korčula Town
MAP E5 ▪ Svetog Roka 2
▪ 020 711 253 ▪ Closed Nov–Mar ▪ KK

This popular seafood restaurant (see p57) in the Old Town is a lively place to eat on a summer night. Grilled fish is the highlight.

(6) Jastožera, Komiža
MAP B5 ▪ Gundulićeva 6
▪ 021 713 253 ▪ KKK

Locally caught lobster is the speciality at this restaurant, but it offers a lot more in the seafood line, too, with fresh fish grilled or baked.

(7) Vila Kaliopa, Vis Town
MAP B5 ▪ Vladimira Nazora 32
▪ 021 711 755 ▪ Closed Oct–Apr ▪ KKK

A treat is in store for diners at this restaurant. Top-notch seafood is served in a sculpture-laden garden in the Kut district of Vis town.

(8) Pojoda, Vis Town
MAP B5 ▪ Don Cvjetka
Marasovića 8 ▪ 021 711 575 ▪ KK

This upmarket restaurant, with an ornate courtyard, charges by the kilo for quality fish. The fine food comes with a wine list and service to match.

(9) Marinero, Korčula Town
MAP E5 ▪ Ulica Marka Andrijića
13 ▪ 020 711 170 ▪ KK

Hidden away down a narrow alley, Marinero serves authentic Dalmatian seafood and quality wines. It's run by two fisherman brothers, so everything is fresh from the sea.

(10) Bistro Palute, Supetar, Brač
MAP C3 ▪ Porat 4 ▪ 021 631 730 ▪ K

Palute offers a large menu of local seafood but has plenty of soups, stews and pasta dishes besides. In summer, tables are placed on a small pier right on Supetar harbour.

See map on pp76–7

⭐ **TOP 10** The Makarska Riviera and Split

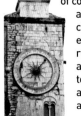

The Makarska Riviera is one of the most picturesque parts of the Dalmatian Coast. Sheltered by the rocky backdrop of the Biokovo mountain range, this long stretch of coast is filled with sandy beaches, lush vegetation and historic towns and cities. Traces of the various civilizations that have swept through the region emerge colourfully, with Roman remnants at the ruined town of Salona, Ottoman strongholds such as the imposing fortress at Klis, and monuments to Venetian rule in Trogir's historic centre. Split, built around the remnants of Diocletian's Palace, is a vibrant and modern metropolis. As Croatia's second biggest city, it is also a busy transport hub, with regular ferries to the nearby islands. This scenically stunning corner of Croatia seems on an inexorable rise.

Clock tower in Diocletian's Palace, Split

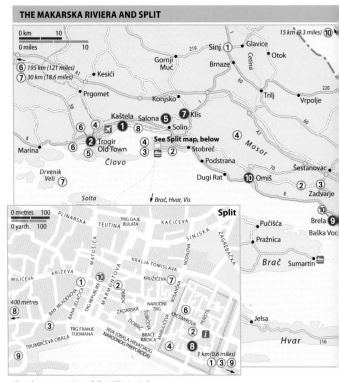

Previous pages Waterfalls in Plitvice Lakes

1 Kaštela

MAP B3 ■ Tourist info: Brce 5, Dvorac Vitturi, Kaštel Lukšić; 021 227 933; www.kastela-info.hr

Between Split and Trogir, an untidy morass of cheap housing and light industry surrounds the main road, but by the coast, the hidden gems of Kaštela await discovery. The "castles" from which the area takes its name date back as far as the 15th century, when they were built both as coastal defences and lavish retreats for the local nobles; you can walk from one to the next along the coast. The highlights are Kaštel Stari (the oldest), which has a decent stretch of beach, pretty Kaštel Gomilica, Kaštel Kambelovac, which has a seafood restaurant, and Kaštel Lukšić, which has been converted into a museum and is close to two beautiful gardens.

The waterfront at Trogir

2 Trogir Old Town

When you've explored the myriad churches, palaces and grand buildings of this perfectly preserved gem *(see pp28–9)*, relax on the wide waterfront Riva, where pavement cafés and alfresco restaurants bubble with activity day and night.

3 Makarska

MAP D4 ■ Tourist info: Obala Kralja Tomislava 16; 021 612 002; www.makarska-info.hr

The pretty port town of Makarska lies within a bay sheltered by the forested St Peter's Peninsula and is one of Dalmatia's liveliest and most popular mainland resorts. The historic centre is full of buildings that date back to Venetian rule, including the Baroque Church of St Mark overlooking the main square. Around the coast, the tone is more lively and modern. Two seafront promenades are lined with bars, restaurants and watersports-hire companies.

A sheltered bay at Makarska

4 Živogošće and Zaostrog

MAP E4 ■ Tourist info: Porat 97; 021 627 077; www.zivogosce.hr

At the southern end of the Makarska Riviera is the small resort of Živogošće. The oldest settlement on this stretch of the coastline, it is home to a 17th-century Franciscan monastery with an impressive Baroque altar and a renowned library, with holdings that shed light on life during the Ottoman occupation of the region. Slightly further south is Zaostrog, home to an older (14th-century) Franciscan monastery with a small art gallery and folk museum.

5 Salona

MAP C3

Salona (the name derives from the Latin word for salt) is the supposed birthplace of Emperor Diocletian *(see p33)*. Nowadays it's just a ruin, with none of the life and energy of Diocletian's Palace, but this old Roman town just outside Split does allow visitors to gain an insight into ancient Roman life. If you can forget the stranglehold of the surrounding industrial development, it's a pretty site, with mountains to one side and the Adriatic to the other. The Tusculum is a good place to begin your exploration. Also look out for the amphitheatre, the Roman baths, the old Forum, the Theatre and the Necropolis of Manastirine.

LANGUAGE AND NATIONHOOD

Under French rule (1806–15), Croatian became the "official" language of Dalmatia, but when the Austrians took over in 1813, they re-introduced Italian as the language of public life – an important spur for the growth of Croatian nationalism. In 1865, Makarska became one of the first communes to bring back Croatian as its official language.

6 Gradac

MAP E4 ■ Tourist info: Trg Soline 11; 021 697 375; www.gradac.hr

Gradac is best known for its beach, which at 6 km (4 miles) is the longest on the Croatian coast *(see p49)*. This spectacular spot has the Biokovo Mountains rising to the north and the islands of Central Dalmatia to the south. There's plenty of shade for the hottest summer days, as well as a campsites and hotels for those who fancy an extended stay.

7 Klis

MAP C3 ■ Tourist info: Megdan 57; 021 240 578; www. tvrdavaklis.com

This hulking fortress complex in the mountains above Split offers impressive views of the area. The Romans were the first to use the site. Later it became a bulwark against the Ottomans, who finally captured it in 1537 after a bitter siege; they held it for more than a century, to the dismay of the residents of Split.

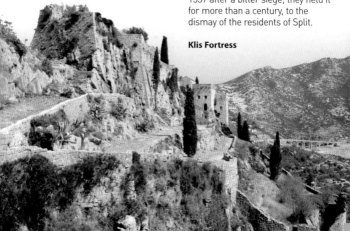

Klis Fortress

8 Diocletian's Palace, Split

Make sure you leave plenty of time to explore and relax in one of the most atmospheric city centres in Europe. The warren-like complex is so captivating that day-trippers often end up missing their ferry or staying an extra day or two. The palace (see pp30–31) is not at all how you expect an ancient monument to be; it's full of life, with people hanging their washing out of the windows of flats set into its walls, bustling restaurants, and funky bars where locals come to see and be seen.

Beautiful shingle beach at Brela

9 Brela

MAP D3 ■ Tourist info: Trg A. Stepinca bb; 021 618 455; www. brela.hr

Travelling south from Split, this is the first resort on the Makarska Riviera, and one of the nicest spots for a day or two by the sea. Brela is a pleasant town with a gaggle of old stone houses and a few modern hotels and restaurants, but it's the pebble and shingle beach that people come for.

10 Omiš

MAP C3 ■ Tourist info: Fošal 1; 021 861 350; www.visitomis.hr

Set at the point where the Cetina river flows into the Adriatic, Omiš is a good base for rafting trips (see p52) and convenient for the gorge and its fish restaurants. Once a notorious pirate bolthole, these days Omiš is a largely modern town, although it does have a small historic quarter, and there are some atmospheric old fortifications in the hills above the town.

THE ENVIRONS OF SPLIT

▶ **MORNING**

Head for the town of **Solin**, just outside **Split**, where the ruins of ancient **Salona** rise above the vineyards and fruit orchards. Don't miss the late Roman basilicas and the 2nd-century amphitheatre. It will take 50–75 minutes to walk the site, so take water and a hat in the height of summer. Grab refreshments in the café at the entrance to the Salona site before heading north to **Klis**, the 10th-century fortress that commands the high ground above Split. Take time to soak up the views from Klis's walls – ramparts that will be familiar to fans of the fantasy series *Game of Thrones* (as the city of Meereen).

Stop for lunch at the Perlica restaurant just north of Klis Fortress. It's famous for it's spit-roast lamb with spring onions.

AFTERNOON

Heading towards Solin, take the old road to Trogir, which passes through the coastal settlement of **Kaštela** (see p87). A sequence of seven linked villages each with its own kaštel or defensive tower, Kaštela is great for a seaside walk, with a coastal path winding its way past small shingle beaches.

Continue to **Trogir** (see pp28–9) for a late-afternoon stroll round the medieval piazzas and alleyways. Reserve at least half an hour for Trogir cathedral, whose stone carving make it an essential sightseeing stop.

A drink on Trogir's waterfront is the perfect way to end the day's tourism.

See map on pp86–7

Beaches

1 Gornja Vala, Gradac
MAP E4

The longest of the Makarska Riviera's pebble beaches is the furthest south, at Gradac. Overlooked by the grey mountains of the Biokovo range, it's a stirring place for a swim.

Gradac on the Makarska Riviera

2 Žnjan, Split
MAP C3

East of central Split, Žnjan is a long pebble beach with cafés, restaurants and facilities for children. The walk from Bačvice to Žnjan along the coastal path (30 minutes) is lovely, whatever the season.

3 Kašjuni, Split
MAP C3s

In a semi-hidden cove below Marjan peninsula, this crescent of fine shingle is a lot quieter than Bačvice. It is a west-facing beach with views of Čiovo island and fine sunsets.

4 Bene, Split
MAP C3

On the northern side of the Marjan peninsula, just beyond the Špinut marina, Bene is a predominantly rocky beach backed by pines. It has good facilities for children.

5 Okrug, Trogir
MAP B3

Just 5 km (3 miles) southeast of Trogir, near the settlement of Okrug Gornji, this 2-km- (1-mile-) long shingle strip dubbed "Copacabana" is hugely popular in the summer. There's a healthy sprinkling of beach bars and watersports facilities.

6 Medena, Trogir
MAPB3

West of Trogir, this long stretch of shingle is backed by bars, restaurants and sports courts. It is a place for seaside walks at all times of year.

7 Krknjaši, Veli Drvenik
MAP B3

Krknjaši Bay is a beautiful inlet with a shallow sandy bottom. There's a bar-restaurant here, and the bay is popular with yachtspeople, but it is still blissfully uncommercialized.

8 Makarska Beach
MAP D4

In the centre of Makarska, there is a beach, almost 2 km (1 mile) long, backed by a line of cafés, restaurants and hotels. There are plenty of sports facilities, too.

9 Bačvice, Split

A broad bay with a shallow sandy floor, Bačvice (see p32) has been a local family favourite. It is famed as the home of picigin, the Dalmatian game in which participants try to prevent a ball from touching the water.

10 Punta Rata, Brela
MAP D3

The Makarska Riviera is famous for its pebble beaches, and Brela's Punta Rata is one of the finest, curving its way around a promontory at the northern end of the resort. It is an excellent place for a paddle.

Punta Rata at Brela

Inland Excursions

① Sinj
MAP C2 ▪ Tourist office:
Put Petrovca 12 ▪ 021 826 352
▪ www.visitsinj.com

A historic mountain town with interesting churches. On the first Sunday in August, Sinj hosts the hugely popular Sinjska Alka knights tournament (which bears similarities to Siena's *Palio*).

② Cetina Gorge
MAP D3

This starkly beautiful gorge cuts through the heart of Central Dalmatia, before a rendezvous with the Adriatic at Omiš. It is increasingly popular with rafters, who often start near the town of Penšići. Foodies savour its fish restaurants.

③ Zadvarje
MAP D3

This village is a good spot for appreciating the beauty of the Cetina Gorge. Nearby, at the Gubavica Falls, the Cetina river plunges dramatically almost 50 m (164 ft) through the karst landscape.

④ Mosor
MAP C3

A mountain range extending between Klis and Omiš, Mosor attractively frames the Cetina river and a number of small villages. Explore it by car, or join the Croatian climbers tackling the barren Mosor Mountain.

⑤ Red Lake and Blue Lake
MAP E3

You cannot see the 300-m- (984-ft-) wide Red Lake (Crveno Jezero), near Imotski, from afar, since it lies in an inaccessible pit. The strange ochre hue of its waters comes from the landscape. It is possible, however, to get down to water level at its sibling, the Blue Lake (Modro Jezero), which takes on a contrasting colour. In summer, low waters reveal bizarre rock formations at this eerie spot.

⑥ Plitvice Lakes
Off MAP ▪ 053 751 015
▪ **Open 7am–8pm daily** ▪ Adm
▪ www.np-plitvicka-jezera.hr

The UNESCO World Heritage listed Plitvice Lakes are an oasis of limestone pools, lakes and waterfalls in a well-organized national park.

The breathtaking Plitvice Lakes

⑦ Krka National Park
MAP A1 ▪ www.npkrka.hr

This spectacular conservation area beside the Krka river is usually entered just above the town of Skradin at Skradinski buk, where boat trips are available for visitors.

⑧ Biokovo Nature Park
MAP D3–E4 ▪ www.pp-biokovo.hr

The jagged ridges of the Biokovo range form one of Croatia's most majestic areas of natural wilderness. You'll have to be an experienced hiker to ascend the seaward slopes.

⑨ Mostar
MAP G3 ▪ Tourist office: +387 (0)36 580 275

This Bosnian city has a famous bridge *(see p71)* on the Neretva river.

⑩ Livno
MAP D2 ▪ www.bhtourism.ba

This southern Bosnian town is renowned for its tasty unpasteurized cheese, which is inexpensive here.

See map on pp86–7

Cafés, Bars and Nightlife

Appetizers at Paradox

① Paradox Wine & Cheese Bar, Split

MAP L1 ■ Ulica bana Jelačića 3

Situated in the historic centre of Split, this wine and cheese bar has a rooftop terrace that offers a great view of the Riva waterfront. It serves amazing Dalmatian wines.

② Luxor, Split

MAP N2 ■ Kraj Sv. Ivana 11

In the heart of Diocletian's Palace, this popular café has an Egyptian-themed interior. There is outdoor seating in the summer.

③ Bačvice, Split

MAP N6

Located south of the centre of Split, this massively popular modern nightlife complex is set on the bay of the same name. There's a multitude of bars, cafés, restaurants and nightclubs to choose from.

④ Academia Club Ghetto, Split

MAP M2 ■ Dosud 10

This retreat of the local cognoscenti gets few tourists as it is on the often-ignored upper level of Diocletian's Palace. It has a busy bar and a spacious courtyard for summer use.

⑤ Deep, Makarska

MAP D4 ■ Šetalište fra Jure Radića 5a

Deep is famed for its extraordinary setting: a tunnel-shaped cave with a beach at the front door. A friendly crowd enjoys eclectic dance-pop.

⑥ Smokvica, Trogir

MAP B3 ■ Radovanov Trg 9

Set in the shadow of the cathedral, this café-bar opens at 7am for espresso and keeps going until the small hours, by which time it has metamorphosed into a buzzing live-music venue with an extensive cocktail menu.

⑦ Pivnica Pivac, Makarska

MAP D4 ■ Marineta 13

This seafront café-bar is one of central Makarska's most popular meeting points. The choice of beers is top-notch, with Croatian craft ales as well as international brands.

⑧ Vidilica, Split

MAP M5 ■ Nazorov prilaz 1

Sweeping views of the city, port and the islands are seen from this café on the Marjan hillside. It is worth the hike on a sunny day just to sit back with a drink and take in the scene.

⑨ Romana, Makarska

MAP D4 ■ Obala kralja Tomislava 21

This is one of the most popular pavement cafés on Makarska's Riva, offering a superb range of cakes and ice creams, as well as good coffee. They make their own chocolates, too.

⑩ Kavana Bajamonti, Split

MAP L2 ■ Trg Republike 1

With its big outdoor terrace, this is one of Split's best spots for coffee, cake and people-watching. It also has a good breakfast menu.

The terrace at Kavana Bajamonti, Split

Places to Eat

PRICE CATEGORIES

For a three-course meal for one with half
a bottle of wine (or equivalent meal),
taxes and extra charges.

K under 150kn   **KK** 150–250kn
KKK over 250kn

 **Stellon, Split**
MAP N6 ▪ Bačvice bb
▪ 021 489 200 ▪ K

A funky favourite with 20- and
30-somethings out at Bačvice,
Stellon offers delicious seafood,
meat dishes, pasta and risotto,
tempting drinks, and wonderful
sea views.

② Noštromo, Split
MAP L2 ▪ Kraj Sv Marije 10
▪ 091 405 6666 ▪ KKK

This smart seafood restaurant
(see p56) is right by the fish market.
Sit upstairs and you can watch as
the ultra-fresh seafood is grilled.

③ Šperun, Split
MAP L2 ▪ Šperun 3
▪ 021 346 999 ▪ KK

Set between the seafront and
hillside Varoš, this charming eatery
serves local specialities in a dining
room filled with antiques and
modern art. It's small but popular,
so it can get crowded.

④ Restoran Riva, Trogir
MAP B3 ▪ Obala bana
Berislavića 15 ▪ 091 582 5931 ▪ KK

Located in Trogir's Old Town, this
restaurant has a terrace that overlooks the Riva. From late April to
November, enjoy the Mediterranean
dishes, pizzas and homemade pasta.

⑤ Stari Mlin, Makarska
MAP D4 ▪ Prvosvibanjska 43
▪ 021 611 509 ▪ KK

Stari Mlin serves delicious Dalmatian
seafood as well as an unusual
selection of fragrant Thai specialities.
It is set in an old stone mill with a
pretty walled garden.

⑥ Konoba Bajamont, Split
MAP M2 ▪ Bajamontijeva 3
▪ 021 355 356 ▪ KK

This little eatery in the Diocletian's
Palace district sticks to traditional
Dalmatian fare. The seafood pasta
and fish dishes are excellently
prepared and never too expensive.

⑦ Villa Spiza, Split
MAP M2 ▪ Kružićeva 3
▪ 091 152 1249 ▪ K

Something of a cult eatery among
Dalmatian foodies, Spiza excels in
traditional stews and seafood dishes,
served in a tiny room. The menu
changes daily based on what is fresh.

The patio at Baletna Škola, Kaštela

⑧ Baletna Škola, Kaštela
MAP B3 ▪ Don Frane Bege 2,
Kaštel Kambelovac ▪ 021 220 208 ▪ K

On the seafront road, this restaurant
enjoys a loyal following among the
locals on account of its excellent
seafood and good inexpensive pizzas.

⑨ Bufet Fife, Split
MAP L2 ▪ Trumbićeva
obala 11 ▪ 021 345 223 ▪ K

This long-standing informal local
favourite serves hearty lunches –
think traditional bean stews and
inexpensive fillets of fish.

⑩ Kalalarga, Makarska
MAP D4 ▪ Kalalarga 3
▪ 098 990 2908 ▪ KK

Combining tradition with a taste for
culinary daring, Kalalarga serves a
trusted menu of fish, seafood and
steaks with the odd innovative twist.

See map on pp86–7

ᴛᴏᴘ10 Southern Dalmatia

Meštrović sculpture at the Račić Mausoleum in Cavtat

Dubrovnik's popularity notwithstanding, Southern Dalmatia remains relatively unexplored and unspoiled. Its appeal lies in the diversity of the natural landscape, with pristine beaches, sheer cliffs, fertile farmland, dense forests, rolling hills and dramatic mountains all in one easily navigable strip of land. The Adriatic is not far away – the generous provider of the quality seafood served in even the most humble *konoba* (taverna), where you may also sample excellent local wines from the vineyards of the Pelješac Peninsula.

Neretva Delta
MAP F5 ▪ Atlas Travel
Agency: 020 642 286 ▪ www.atlas-croatia.com

On its journey to the sea, the Neretva river fans out to create the lush, water-drenched landscape of the Neretva Delta. This 200-sq-km (77-sq-mile) expanse is partially navigable by boat, and can also

The lush Neretva Delta

SOUTHERN DALMATIA

[Map of Southern Dalmatia showing locations including Hvar, Sućuraj, Zaostrog, Gradac, Čapljina, Vid, Neretva Delta, Ploče, Metković, Lovište, Duba Plješka, Trpanj, Blace, Opuzen, Viganj, Orebić, Korčula, Korčula Town, Blato, Pelješac Vineyards, Klek, Hutovo, Neum, Žuljana, Pelješac Peninsula, Ston, Mali Ston, Lastovo Town, Polače, Kozarica, Mljet National Park, Šipanska Luka, Ubli, Lastovo, Mljet, Sobra, Korita, Šipan, Adriatic Sea]

0 km   15
0 miles   15

be explored by car. Not only is the delta vital to Croatian agriculture, it provides a sanctuary for the myriad species of bird that stop off here as they migrate south to Africa. Many fish inhabit this angler's paradise, including eels and trout. The Atlas Travel Agency organize visits from Dubrovnik.

2 Peljašac Vineyards
MAP E5

Many people treat the Peljašac Peninsula as little more than a quick route from Dubrovnik to Korčula town. In doing so, they miss an opportunity to explore the vineyards that produce what is arguably Croatia's best red wine, Dingač. A guided tour is a simple way of rectifying this oversight; Atlas's Dubrovnik-based excursion takes in a wine cellar in the village of Potomje. From Potomje, tunnels bored into the Peljašac mountains lead to quiet beaches.

The harbour at Orebić

3 Orebić
MAP E5 ■ Tourist info: Zrinsko-Frankopanska 2 ■ 020 713 718 ■ www.visitorebic-croatia.hr

The small seaside town of Orebić, on the Peljašac Peninsula, has been luring visitors for decades, with its idyllic location, long pebble beaches, laid-back cafés and restaurants. Luxurious apartments in the town are an alternative to the nearby hotels.

4 Ston
MAP F6 ■ Tourist info: Peljaški put 1 ■ 020 754 452 ■ www.ston.hr

The Republic of Ragusa (see pp12–13) left an enduring reminder of its presence in Ston. The 14th-century fortifications, built to guard against attack by sea, resemble a miniature Great Wall of China. Today's relaxed pace of life is a far cry from the days when Ston was the second most powerful centre in the Republic. Other attractions include salt pans, and stunning views of the Dinaric Mountains and the peaks of Bosnia-Herzegovina.

| 1 Top 10 Sights see pp94–7 |
| 1 Restaurants see p101 |
| 1 Bars and Wineries see p100 |
| 1 The Best of the Rest see p98 |
| 1 Beaches see p99 |

Fortifications at Ston

5 Mali Ston
MAP G6

A short walk north of Ston is its smaller sibling Mali Ston. Gastronomes from all over Croatia and Italy flock to "Little Ston" for the finest fresh fish, with shellfish plucked straight from the Malostonski Channel seen as a highlight on any menu. The scenery is as spectacular as the seafood, and it is no surprise that this idyllic spot has become a popular haunt with amorous Croatian weekenders.

6 Trsteno Arboretum
MAP G6 ■ Potok 20, Trsteno ■ 020 751 019 ■ Open May–Oct: 7am–7pm daily; Nov–Apr: 8am–4pm daily ■ Adm

At the beginning of the 16th century, the Gučetić family built a summer retreat overlooking the coast at Trsteno and gave it a beautiful Renaissance garden. The garden still survives in something approaching its original shape and has been expanded to form one of Europe's most impressive arboretums. This collection of trees and plants from around the world tumbles towards the Adriatic, with fine views of Trsteno harbour and the Elafiti Islands beyond. One of the highlights

Sculpture at the Račić Mausoleum in Cavtat

of this tranquil oasis is a water garden with an ornate fountain depicting Neptune surrounded by nymphs.

NEUM

The road between Split and Dubrovnik passes through a 9-km (6-mile) stretch of coast owned by Bosnia-Herzegovina. This strip of land was originally given to the Ottoman Empire in 1699 to create a buffer between the Republic of Ragusa's territory and that of its rival Venice. Neum later became part of Bosnia. Visitors will have to stop here to show their passports to officials.

7 Cavtat
MAP H7 ■ Bukovac House: Vlahe Bukovca 5 ■ 020 478 646 ■ Apr–Oct: 9am–6pm Mon–Sat, 9am–2pm Sun; Nov–Mar: 10am–6pm Tue–Sat, 9am–1pm Sun ■ Adm

First inhabited in the 3rd century BC, this resort still bears the marks of the Illyrians, Greeks, Romans and Slavs who have occupied it. Look for the 16th-century Rector's Palace, and a mausoleum designed by Ivan Meštrović. Also worth a visit is Bukovac House, dedicated to the memory of one of Croatia's most famous painters.

Fountain at Trsteno Arboretum, with Neptune as its focus

8 Sokol grad
MAP J7 ■ Dunave ■ 020 638 800 ■ Open Apr & May: 10am–6pm; Jun–Oct: 10am–7pm; Nov: 10am–4pm; Dec–Mar: noon–3pm ■ Adm

Overlooked by stark grey mountains, Sokol grad ("Hawk Castle") sprouts from a fist-shaped clump of rock. A fortress since prehistoric times, this was an important part of Dubrovnik Republic's frontier defences at times of Ottoman attack. This much-visited attraction has great views from its ramparts and a rewarding display of medieval military hardware inside.

Mljet National Park

9 Mljet National Park
MAP E6 ■ Pristanište 2, Goveđari ■ 020 744 041 ■ www.np-mljet.hr ■ Adm (children free)

The western corner of Mljet was designated a National Park in 1960 to conserve the island's holm oak and Aleppo pine forests. Among the main attractions are the interconnected saltwater lakes, Veliko Jezero ("Great Lake") and Malo Jezero ("Small Lake"). The islet of St Mary, in Veliko Jezero, is home to a 12th-century Benedictine monastery. Another highlight is the village of Polače, with its Roman ruins astride the harbour.

10 Lastovo
MAP D6 ■ Tourist info: Pjevor 7; 020 801 018; www.tz-lastovo.hr

Reached by summer-only catamaran from Dubrovnik or regular ferry from Split, Lastovo is less visited than Southern Dalmatia's other islands. The main settlement, Lastovo town, is on a steep inland hillside, many of its streets akin to stone stairways. Zaklopatica bay boasts a couple of excellent seafood restaurants.

THE ELAPHITE ISLANDS

This itinerary is based on the summer ferry timetable (Jun–Sep), which makes it possible to visit three islands in one day. At other times of year, one or two islands is more realistic.

▶ MORNING

After coffee in one of the seafront cafes on **Gruž Harbour**, take the 10am ferry to **Koločep** (see p98), arriving at the island's small harbour 30 minutes later. You have 4 hours before your next departure, which is plenty of time to explore the island's clifftop paths or loll on Koločep's smooth sandy beach. Opt for a lunch of squid or fish in one of the harbour-front restaurants, keeping a watchful eye on the arrival of your next ferry connection.

AFTERNOON

The 2:35pm ferry whisks you from Koločep to **Lopud** (see p98), leaving you with roughly 2½ hours to stroll around the **Đorđić-Mayneri Park** (see p61), take a peek at the **Church of Our Lady of the Rocks** (see p44), and jump aboard a golf-cart taxi to the fabulous beach at **Šunj** (see p99). Your ferry to Suđurad on the south coast of **Šipan** (see p98) leaves Lopud at 5:30pm, giving you 45 minutes to look around once you arrive – just enough time to amble around its attractive harbour and admire the fortified Renaissance villa of the Skočibuha family. Leaving Suđurad at 6:30pm, your final ferry of the day provides a leisurely journey along the South Dalmatian coast, arriving back in Dubrovnik just in time for dinner.

See map on pp94–5 ←

The Best of the Rest

Viganj
MAP E5

This small settlement with a 17th-century Dominican monastery unfolds around the Bay of Viganj, backed by the Pelješac mountains and looking out to the island of Korčula. Windsurfers flock to this picturesque spot for its reliably windswept beaches.

Performance in the centre of Čilipi

Čilipi
MAP H7

With regular folk events and an ethnographic museum, Čilipi is on the tour circuit from Dubrovnik. On Sundays during high season, the presence of performers in traditional costumes brightens up the main square.

3 Vid
MAP F5

Inhabited by both Greeks and Romans, Vid thrived as a trading post between the islands and the hinterland until the 7th century AD. View the remains of Roman Narona throughout the town, as well as at Vid's museum.

4 Janjina
MAP F5

This compact village, with an ornate church, tumbles down the Pelješac hillside towards the sea. It's a great place for wine from local vineyards.

Koločep
MAP G6

One of the Elafiti Islands, Koločep is mainly renowned for a sandy beach that is seldom as crowded as Dubrovnik's, a short ferry ride away. There are two small villages to explore, as well as the dense woods that cover most of the island.

Bačina Lakes
MAP F5

These six interlinked freshwater lakes just north of Ploče are an impressive sight. Surrounded by lush vegetation, they provide a habitat for a plethora of fish and bird species.

7 Lopud
MAP G6

Once a populous stronghold of the Republic of Ragusa, Lopud now enjoys a peaceful retirement. An old monastery, churches and a choice of beaches make this Elafiti island worth a visit.

8 Trpanj
MAP E5 ▪ Tourist office: Žalo 7 ▪ 020 743 433 ▪ www.tzo-trpanj.hr

The Pelješac Peninsula's north coast is the picturesque setting for a small resort with a pebble beach and a cluster of pavement cafés. Trpanj affords sweeping views across Malo More towards the Biokovo Mountains.

9 Trstenik
MAP F5

On the east coast of the Pelješac Peninsula you can visit relaxed Trstenik, known for its old stone houses and a sheltered harbour. Protected by the hills that rear up behind it, the village has seaward views of Mljet and Lastovo.

10 Šipan
MAP G6

The largest of the Elafiti Islands is also the richest in monuments such as churches and fortresses.

See map on pp94–5

Beaches

1 **Kupari**
MAP H6

This crescent of shingle is one of the finest beaches in Dubrovnik, with crystal clear water and picturesque views.

2 **Srebreno**
Immediately east of Kupari, Srebreno *(see p71)* is a shallow semicircular bay bordered by boating piers and shingle beaches. There are cafés along the seafront and a luxury hotel looms just above.

3 **Šunj, Lopud**
MAP G6

This mixture of shingle and sand stretches across a bay on the eastern side of Lopud island, looking back towards Koločep and Dubrovnik. The path to Šunj from Lopud harbour takes you through some lovely untouched island scenery.

4 **Koločep**
MAP G6

A ferry ride from Dubrovnik, Koločep boasts a small but pretty curve of sandy beach a short walk from the ferry harbour. There's a hotel behind the beach offering café, restaurant and beach-hire facilities.

5 **Drače**
MAP F5

With stretches of pebble spread either side of the small village harbour, the north-facing beaches of Drače offer splendid views of the mountainous Dalmatian mainland.

6 **Trstenica, Orebić**
MAP E5

One of the Pelješac Peninsula's most popular family beaches, Trstenica is a grand sweep of fine shingle with views of Korčula island. The beach is at the end of Orebić seafront, which is lined with cafés and restaurants.

7 **Punta, Viganj**
MAP E5

A pebbly spit reaching into the Korčula channel, Punta is favoured by windsurfers but also has plenty of space for sunbathers and swimmers. Buzzing beach bars are just inland.

8 **Papratno, Ston**
MAP F6

Just 3 km (2 miles) west of Ston, Papratno beach is a long strip of fine shingle washed by warm, clear seas. There's a large campsite with plenty of eating and drinking facilities, and a nearby harbour for ferries to Mljet.

9 **Vučine, Žuljana**
MAP F5

A few minutes' walk from Žuljana village, this fine strip of pebble is surrounded by greenery and over-looked by steep, maquis-covered slopes. Facing west, it's a great place for sunsets.

10 **Divna, Trpanj**
MAP E5

You'll need your own transport to get to Divna, a secluded shingle beach at the end of a ravine west of Trpanj. You won't be entirely alone: there's a small campsite and a rudimentary beach bar for refreshments.

Pretty Divna beach, Trpanj

Bars and Wineries

The vaulted tasting room at Korta Katarina Winery, Orebić

1 Korta Katarina Winery, Orebić
MAP E5 ■ Bana Jelačića 3 ■ 020 713 817

This winery just outside Orebić makes outstanding reds from its own vineyards and dry whites from grapes harvested in Korčula. There's also a wine bar, tasting room and shop.

2 K2, Viganj
MAP E5 ■ Viganj bb ■ Closed Oct–Apr

There's a day-long buzz at this open-air bar behind Punta Beach, often packed with windsurfers. Nights see a flurry of DJs and live music.

3 Vertigo, Srebreno
MAP H6 ■ Dr F Tuđmana 20

Overlooking the sea, 10 km (6 miles) southeast of Dubrovnik, this popular spot is a café by day and a club by night. It has a range of guest DJs.

4 Riva, Cavtat
MAP H7

While away a pleasant hour or so at one of the café-bars on Cavtat's waterfront, taking in the distinctly Mediterranean ambience and the views over the bay and islands.

5 Villa Ruža, Koločep
MAP G6 ■ Donje Čelo bb ■ 020 757 030 ■ Closed Oct–Apr

A 30-minute ferry ride from Dubrovnik, this relaxing lounge bar offers delicious cocktails and beautiful sea views.

6 Saints Hills Winery, Trpanj
MAP E5 ■ Oskorušno ■ 020 742 113 ■ Open 11am–5pm by appt ■ Dinner from 7pm (booking essential)

This impressive winery in an old farmhouse also has a gourmet, reservation-only restaurant.

7 Skaramuča Wine Bar, Pijavičino
MAP E5 ■ Pijavičino 7 ■ 020 742 211

Pijavičino is inland from Skaramuča's hillside-hugging vineyards at Dingač. You can taste and buy their famous velvety wine at this roadside spot.

8 Peninsula Wine Bar, Donja Banda
MAP E5 ■ Donja Banda bb ■ 098 285 824

In a village on the main Orebić–Ston road, this welcoming bar serves pretty much everything grown in the vineyards of the Pelješac Peninsula and neighbouring Korčula.

9 Waterfront, Orebić
MAP E5

After a day on one of Dalmatia's best beaches (see pp48–9), unwind further in one of Orebić's waterfront cafés, with great views of Korčula.

10 Konoba Karmela, Viganj
MAP E5 ■ Viganj 36

With a shady wooden terrace over the water, this bar/eatery is popular with locals. Great for coffee, beer, wine or a light Dalmatian meal.

Restaurants

PRICE CATEGORIES

For a three-course meal for one with half
a bottle of wine (or equivalent meal),
taxes and extra charges.

K under 150kn   KK 150–250kn
KKK over 250kn

1 Vila Koruna, Mali Ston
MAP G6 ▪ Mali Ston
▪ 020 754 999 ▪ K

Arguably the best choice in a small
town that boasts a number of first-
class fish restaurants, Vila Koruna
(see p56). is a must for seafood lovers.
It is also a popular romantic spot

2 Kapetanova Kuća, Mali Ston
MAP G6 ▪ Mali Ston ▪ 020 754 555
▪ KK

Another popular Mali Ston eatery,
Kapetanova Kuća serves up mussels
taken straight from the Malostonski
Channel, fish grills and Pelješac
wine. The seafood risotto is divine.

3 Bugenvila, Cavtat
MAP H7 ▪ Obala dr. Ante
Starčevića 9 ▪ 020 479 949 ▪ KK

Bugenvila *(see p56)* offers imaginative
Mediterranean cuisine with laid-back
ambience and superb service. The
seasonal menu focuses on fresh
seafood and creative desserts.
Quite pricey, but well worth it.

4 Vrgorac, Orebić
MAP E5 ▪ Perna 24
▪ 020 719 152 ▪ K

With wooden tables on a leafy
terrace, and views across the sea
channel to Korčula Island, Vrgorac
serves excellent Dalmatian seafood
and local wines.

5 Kolona, Cavtat
MAP H7 ▪ Put Tihe 2
▪ 020 478 787 ▪ Closed Nov–Mar ▪ KK

Kolona charms with its grilled fish,
attentive service and long lasting
tradition. Innovative dishes have
crept onto a largely Dalmatian menu.

6 Augusta Insula, Lastovo Town
MAP D6 ▪ Zaklopatica 21 ▪ 098 938
6035 ▪ Closed Nov–Apr ▪ KK

One of the best restaurants on
Lastovo, this is a hit with the sailing
crowd, who can moor up outside
and enjoy the exquisite seafood.

7 Ogigija, Mljet
MAP F6 ▪ Polače 17 ▪ 020 744
090 ▪ Closed Oct–Apr ▪ KK

The emphasis is on fish at this pension
and restaurant, which has a large
terrace looking out over the sea.

8 Bakus, Ston
MAP F6 ▪ Angeli Radovani 5
▪ 020 754 270 ▪ KK

Mixing traditional Dalmatian cooking
with high culinary standards, this is
the perfect spot *(see p56)* for local
shellfish and some unique desserts.

Superb seafood at Bakus

9 Gverović-Orsan, Zaton Mali
MAP H6 ▪ Štikovica 43 ▪ 020 891 267
▪ Closed Dec–Mar ▪ KKK

This excellent little restaurant, just
a short drive north of Dubrovnik,
serves quality fresh seafood right
by the Adriatic on its terrace.

10 Koraćeva Kuća, Gruda
MAP J7 ▪ Gruda bb ▪ 020 791
557 ▪ Closed mid-Oct–mid-Apr ▪ KK

Come here for locally sourced meat
dishes cooked the traditional way –
either roasted in an ember-covered
pot or grilled over a charcoal fire.

See map on pp94–5

Streetsmart

Onofrio's Large Fountain, Dubrovnik

Getting To and Around Dubrovnik and the Dalmatian Coast

Arriving by Air

Two airports serve the Dalmatian coast: one is in **Dubrovnik**, and one in **Split**. The island of Brač also has a smaller airport, close to the town of Bol, which is mainly used for charter traffic from Europe, especially during the summer season. You can also fly to Croatia's capital, Zagreb, and pick up a **Croatia Airlines** connecting flight to Dubrovnik or Split from there.

Dubrovnik airport is located 22 km (14 miles) southeast of the city, just beyond the coastal town of Cavtat. Regular buses run from the airport into Dubrovnik – dropping passengers at the Pile Gate, the main western entrance to the Old City, before proceeding to the bus terminal on Dubrovnik's western outskirts. Be aware that the pick-up location on the route towards the airport from Dubrovnik is different. Buses stop near the cable-car station instead of the Pile Gate.

An increasing number of international airlines fly to Dubrovnik, including British Airways and a few budget airlines.

Split airport is 20 km (12 miles) west of town between Kaštela and Trogir. There is a bus service from the airport to Split bus station. Among the airlines flying to Split are **British Airways**, **Jet2**, **easyJet** and **Wizzair**.

Arriving by Rail

Dubrovnik does not have a railway connection. The nearest station is at Split, which is connected to the European rail network via Zagreb. Split's train station is in the centre of the city, a 5-minute walk from the Diocletian's Palace area. Split is 4–5 hours from Dubrovnik by car or bus.

Arriving by Bus

Dubrovnik Bus Station is 2 km (1 mile) west of the centre at Kantafig. Buses 1A and 1B run from here to the Pile Gate, the main entrance to the Old City. The bus station is served by several daily intercity buses from Zagreb, Split and elsewhere in Croatia. There are also daily international arrivals from Bosnia-Herzegovina, Montenegro and Germany.

Split Bus Station, next to the train station, is another major transport hub, with daily arrivals from all over Croatia, as well as from a number of German and Italian cities.

Arriving by Ferry

Dubrovnik and Split are Dalmatia's main entry points for international ferries, although there are a number of seasonal crossings from Italy to the Dalmatian Islands.

Dubrovnik's ferry port is at Gruž, 4 km (2 miles) west of the Old City, to which it is linked by buses 1A and 1B. It is served by

ferry from the Italian port of Bari one to four times a week from late March to late November. The crossing takes 8–10 hours and usually runs overnight, although there is often a daytime sailing once per week in high season. Split's ferry port is next to the train and bus stations on the eastern edge of the town centre. It is served by **Jadrolinija** ferries from Ancona (10–11 hours) by two ferries a week in Nov–Mar, and four ferries a week in August, and three ferries a week during rest of the months. In summer there is a 4-hour **SNAV** ferry from Ancona.

If you are aiming straight for the islands, Stari Grad on Hvar is served by Jadrolinija ferries from Ancona (Aug), and by SNAV passenger-only catamaran from Pescara.

Arriving by Road

Dubrovnik lies at the extreme south of Croatia, and getting here can be time consuming, whatever your point of departure might be. If you are travelling from or through Italy, you can use one of the Bari–Dubrovnik or Ancona–Split ferries. Otherwise, the A1 Zagreb–Split–Ploče toll motorway is the quickest option; however, it ends 123 km (76 miles) north of Dubrovnik, and the final stretch involves a tiring but scenic drive on the winding coastal highway. Only a person with a valid driving licence highway. Only a person with a valid driving licence issued in Croatia or an international driving licence may operate a motor vehicle.

Travelling by Bus

Public transport in Dubrovnik is provided by the **Libertas** city bus service, with quick and effective links between main points. Services usually run until midnight (2am in summer). Single-journey tickets cost 12kn from a kiosk or 15kn from the driver.

As there are no trains along the coast, intercity buses provide best means of getting around Dalmatia. Dubrovnik, Makarska and Split all have well-organized bus stations with timetable information and ticket counters. Smaller towns have a bus shelter beside the road – passengers boarding here pay the driver.

There is a bus from Dubrovnik to Split roughly every hour (with a journey time of 4–5 hours). Each of the main islands has a local bus service.

Travelling by Car

No vehicles are allowed inside Dubrovnik's Old City except for delivery vans, which are given access for a few hours every morning. Streets elsewhere in the centre are narrow, parking spaces are hard to find, and the one-way system is trying for the first-time visitor. It is far better to leave your car at the parking garage at Ilijina Glavica, just uphill from the Old City, and walk to the Pile Gate.

It is advisable to check on **HAK (Croatian Automobile Club)**, a real-time information website for traffic conditions.

The main highway (Jadranska magistrala) that runs up the coast from Dubrovnik to Split can be very busy, but it provides a scenic journey.

Cars are allowed on the major islands, but it is expensive to transport them there by ferry and often cheaper to hire a vehicle on arrival.

Travelling by Taxi

In Dubrovnik, taxis are a useful way to shuttle between the Old City, the port at Gruž, and the hotels of Lapad peninsula and Babin Kuk. **Dubrovnik taxi** ranks are outside the western and eastern entrances to the Old City. **Split taxi** ranks can be found at the train and bus stations, as well as on the seafront Riva.

Travelling by Bicycle

Hilly Dubrovnik and crowded Split are far from ideal destinations for the urban cyclist. It is a different story on the islands, with easy cycling in the coastal towns, well-marked trails in the hinterland, and plenty of places to rent bikes.

DIRECTORY

ARRIVING BY AIR

British Airways
W britishairways.com

Croatia Airlines
W croatiaairlines.com

Dubrovnik Airport
MAP H7
C 020 773 100
W airport-dubrovnik.hr

easyJet
W easyjet.com

Jet2
W jet2.com

Split Airport
MAP B3
C 021 203 507
W split-airport.hr

Wizzair
W wizzair.com

ARRIVING BY RAIL

Croatian Train Information
C 060 333 444

ARRIVING BY BUS

Dubrovnik Bus Station
MAP J8
◼ Obala Ivana Pavla II 44A
C 060 305 070

Split Bus Station
MAP N6
◼ Obala kneza Domagoja 12
C 021 329 180
W ak-split.hr

ARRIVING BY FERRY

Jadrolinija (Split)
C 021 338 333
W jadrolinija.hr

SNAV (Italy)
C +39 081 428 5555
W snav.it

TRAVELLING BY BUS

Libertas
W libertasdubrovnik.hr

TRAVELLING BY CAR

HAK Information Centre
C 072 777 777
W hak.hr

TRAVELLING BY TAXI

Dubrovnik Taxi
C 020 411 411

Split Taxi
C 021 473 737

Practical Information

Passports and Visas

Citizens of EU countries, the United States, Canada, Australia, New Zealand, Japan and South Korea can enter Croatia visa-free for up to 90 days within any 180-day period. Visitors from countries other than those listed above may require a visa; check the website of the **Croatian Ministry of Foreign Affairs** for a list of countries whose citizens require visas. If you do need one, seek advice from the Croatian embassy in your home country.

All foreign visitors are required to register with the local police within 48 hours. In practice, this is almost always done for you by your hotel, campsite or accommodation host, so you should not need to worry about this formality.

Most countries have consular representation in Croatia, including **Australia**, **UK** and the **US**.

People travelling with animals must ensure that their pet has an International Pet Passport, is microchipped, and has up-to-date documentation of all vaccinations. Dogs must be vaccinated for rabies at least 21 days before entry.

Customs and Immigration

There are no restrictions on the personal effects brought into Croatia by citizens of EU member states except the following: 800 cigarettes, 200 cigars, 10 litres of spirits, and 90 litres of wine. Non-EU citizens can bring in or take out 200 cigarettes or 50 cigars, 1 litre of spirits, 2 litres of wine, and 50 millilitres of perfume or essence.

On entering the country, all major high-value items such as expensive radios, TVs, computers or photographic equipment should be declared. An unlimited amount of foreign or Croatian currency can be taken in and out of the country by EU citizens. Non-EU visitors should declare cash or cheques amounting to more than €10,000 or equivalent.

Travel Safety Advice

Visitors can get up-to-date travel safety information from the **UK Foreign and Commonwealth Office**, **US Department of State** and the **Australian Department of Foreign Affairs and Trade**.

Travel Insurance

All travellers are advised to buy insurance against accidents, illness, theft or loss, and cancellations. Croatia has a reciprocal health agreement with all EU countries, but EU citizens must have a valid European Health Insurance Card (EHIC) in order to receive any necessary treatment under the public health-care system. Treatment is free for bearers of an EHIC, but medicines and materials must be paid for. Non-EU visitors will pay for all treatment, unless their country has reciprocal arrangements with Croatia.

Health

Croatia has a state health service with a developed infrastructure. Health professionals are highly trained, and facilities are, on the whole, up to date, although Croatia's hospitals are often overcrowded, gloomy and frequently suffer from poor signage – you might have to ask for the department you need.

In Dubrovnik, the **General Hospital** on the Lapad peninsula, at the end of bus route No. 9, deals with walk-in patients and is also the site of the city's main Accident & Emergency (ER) department. In Split, the same job is done by the **Clinical-Hospital Centre** at Firule.

Smaller towns and the larger Adriatic islands are served by a health centre (Dom zdravlja), which will deal with most minor complaints but will transfer you to Split or Dubrovnik in the case of a serious ailment. Medicines can be bought at a pharmacy (ljekarna). Croatian pharmacies are reasonably well stocked, although you should bring sufficient supplies of any prescription drugs you are currently taking. If you run out or lose these, you will have to go to a Croatian hospital or health centre in order to get a new prescription.

Personal Security

Croatia is generally a safe place, and crime rates are relatively low. Keeping you and your possessions secure is largely down to common sense. Don't leave unattended valuables on the beach; don't leave the windows or balcony doors of your apartment or hotel room open if you have left anything of value inside; and beware of pickpockets in crowded places such as markets or on public transport. Few parts of Dubrovnik or Southern Dalmatia are dangerous at night.

There are no designated lost-property offices in Dalmatia, and, if you lose anything, your first point of enquiry should be the local police station. Local restaurants and transport companies are usually good about keeping items that have been left behind.

Traffic can be a hazard to pedestrians in built-up areas: main roads are frequently badly lit, the boundary between pavement and roadway is often indistinct, and in many cases the pavement is simply nonexistent.

Emergency Services

Police, fire brigade and ambulance services can all be reached by dialling the same **emergency number**. The number also covers the mountain rescue service (HGSS), which helps those who encounter difficulties while hiking or climbing in the Dalmatian highlands, as well as a maritime rescue service that performs the same function for those at sea.

Women Travellers

Dubrovnik and Southern Dalmatia are quite safe for women on their own. Patriarchal values still rule in the more rustic parts of Dalmatia, but a more cosmopolitan culture is the norm in urban areas and places that have been touched by tourism.

Travellers with Specific Needs

Getting around Southern Dalmatia can be difficult for wheelchair users. Dubrovnik's Old City is full of stepped streets that are only partially served by ramps, making much of it inaccessible. The central street of Stradun and its neighbouring alleys are accessible, however.

Travelling to the islands requires a degree of forward planning. Wheelchair access to the smaller passenger-only ferries and catamarans is problematic due to their narrow gangways, so you should enquire at the ticket desk as to which vessels are accessible.

The larger car ferries between Split and the major islands have lifts available for use by wheelchair passengers. Some of the popular beaches (including Bačvice and Žnjan in Split) are equipped with wheelchair ramps.

Zajednica saveza osoba s invaliditetom Hrvatske (The Association of Organizations of Disabled People in Croatia) operates across Croatia, and can provide a wealth of useful information for travellers with specific needs.

DIRECTORY

PASSPORTS AND VISAS

Australia
C 02 6286 6988
W au.mvep.hr

Croatian Ministry of Foreign and European Affairs
W mvep.hr

UK
C 020 7387 2022
W uk.mvep.hr

US
C 202 588 5899
W us.mvep.hr

TRAVEL SAFETY ADVICE

Australia
Australian Department of Foreign Affairs and Trade
W dfat.gov.au
W smartraveller.gov.au

UK
Foreign and Commonwealth Office
W gov.uk/foreign-travel-advice

US
US Department of State
W travel.state.gov

HEALTH

Clinic-Hospital Centre, Split
MAP N6 Klinički bolnički centar Split
C 021 556 111
W kbsplit.hr

General Hospital, Dubrovnik
Map J8 • Opća Bolnica Dubrovnik C 020 431 777
W bolnica-du.hr

EMERGENCY SERVICES

Police, Fire, Ambulance, Mountain Rescue and Sea Rescue
C 112

TRAVELLERS WITH SPECIFIC NEEDS

Zajednica saveza osoba s invaliditetom Hrvatske
C 01 482 9394
W soih.hr

Currency and Banking

Croatia's currency is the kuna (written either kn or HRK). One kuna consists of 100 lipa. The currency comes in 5-, 10-, 20- and 50-lipa coins; 1-, 2- and 5-kuna coins; and 10-, 20-, 50-, 100-, 200-, 500- and 1,000-kuna notes.

Prices of goods and services in the tourist industry are sometimes quoted in euros, but payment must be made in kuna. It is highly unlikely that shops, cafés or restaurants will accept euros, so it is important to buy local currency before or as soon as you arrive.

ATMs, banks and bureaux de change (mjenjačnice) are easy to find in Dubrovnik, Split and Southern Dalmatia's main resorts. Using international credit and debit cards to get local currency out of ATMs ensures that you don't have to bring much cash with you, but it will incur minor costs imposed by your bank at home and may involve a slightly lower exchange rate than you would get if you changed cash in a bank or bureau de change. Most banks and exchange bureaux will change cash without commission.

Credit and debit cards are accepted by most shops, restaurants, hotels and travel agencies.

Telephone and Internet

Most apartments, hostels and hotels, as well as a growing number of cafés and restaurants, now offer free Wi-Fi internet access to their guests. The sheer ubiquity of Wi-Fi has led to the almost total demise of internet cafés in urban areas.

With the costs of international roaming being abolished within the EU, visitors from EU countries will be able to use their mobile phones (and access the internet from them) in Croatia for around the same price as they do at home. Visitors from outside the EU should check with their operator what the likely cost of calls and data usage will be. If you have a smartphone equipped with Skype, you can use one of the locally available Wi-Fi networks to make calls that way. If you are spending a long time in the country, you could consider buying a prepaid Croatian SIM card, which can be topped up by buying vouchers from newspaper kiosks or post offices.

Postal Services

The Croatian national postal service – Hrvatska Pošta, or HP – operates a network of post offices, with branches in all towns. Each office offers a wide range of services, from the sale of stamps, envelopes and packaging, to fax services and money exchange. Post offices also sell top-up vouchers for Croatian mobile phones and for mobile internet services. Stamps for postcards and letters can also be bought from newspaper kiosks. Standard letters and postcards to the UK usually take 5–7 days, and 10–14 days to North America and Australasia. If you need to send something quickly and securely in Croatia itself, Hrvatska Pošta's HP Express service is the best option.

Dubrovnik and **Split main post offices** are open 7am–8pm Monday to Friday, and 8am–3pm on Saturday. Smaller branches in Southern Dalmatian towns and on the islands have slightly shorter opening hours.

Television and Radio

The Voice of Croatia is the international department of Croatian National Radio, broadcasting news and comment in English and other languages on their satellite station.

Most apartments and hotel rooms come with both Croatian and international TV channels, possibly including English-language news stations. Local Croatian TV channels broadcast a large selection of films, dramas and sitcoms in English with Croatian subtitles.

Newspapers and Magazines

Croatia's main daily newspapers are *Jutarnji List*, *Večernji List* and the Dalmatia-based *Slobodna Dalmacija*. Influential weekly news magazines include *Globus* and *Nacional*. Although *Slobodna Dalmacija* publishes an occasional English-language supplement called the *Adriatic Times*, there is a lack of English-language print media in Croatia. ***Time Out Croatia*** publishes a magazine-format guide once a year and has a useful website.

Major English-language newspapers are available from newspaper kiosks in central Dubrovnik, Split and Hvar town a day or two after their publication at home. There are also plenty of international magazines on sale, especially those covering popular interests.

Opening Hours

Shops are usually open 8am–8pm Monday to Friday, and 8am–3pm Saturday. These hours are often longer in summer, but some shops close for a few hours in the afternoon when temperatures are at their highest. Supermarkets usually stay open for longer on Saturdays, as well as for a few hours on Sundays.

Banks are usually open 8am–5pm Monday to Friday (some as late as 7pm), and from 8am to 1 or 2pm on Saturday. Private exchange bureaux have longer hours, especially in more touristy areas.

Early-morning coffee drinkers should note that cafés and bars are usually open from around 7am, although they may start earlier if they are located near a busy bus station or ferry terminal.

Many museums and galleries are closed at least one day a week, usually Monday.

Time Difference

Croatia is on Central European Time (CET), 1 hour ahead of GMT, 6 hours ahead of US Eastern Standard Time, and 11 hours behind Australian Eastern Standard Time. The clock comes forward one hour on the last Sunday in March, and back one hour on the last Sunday in October.

Electrical Appliances

The electric current is 220 volts. Many electrical appliances such as hair dryers have 110/220-volt transformers built in, so converters may be less of a concern if you are coming from North America. But be sure to bring an adapter with two round pins.

Driving

Croatia recognizes UK, Australian, Canadian and US driving licences. Drivers should carry their full and valid licence, registration and insurance documents. To hire a car in Croatia, you must be at least 21 years of age.

Weather

Southern Dalmatia enjoys a Mediterranean climate characterized by hot dry summers and mild dry winters. Temperatures can be very high in July and August, when you are advised to wear a hat, carry plenty of water and make good use of your sun cream. In Dubrovnik, the sea can sometimes be warm enough to swim from May to October. Spring and early autumn are the ideal seasons to indulge in urban sightseeing, hiking or cycling, since they usually provide sunny weather and mild temperatures.

One feature of the Dalmatian climate to be aware of is the wind. The Jugo is a warm southerly wind that brings blustery conditions and choppy seas, quickly emptying the beaches. The less frequent but far stronger Bura is a northerly gale that sometimes results in the suspension of catamaran-ferry services, and speed restrictions on main roads.

In summer you will need light cotton clothing with a jacket or pullover for the evenings, plus swimwear. In winter you will need woollen jumpers and a warm coat. Be sure to pack at least one decent pair of walking shoes, as some of the region's medieval towns have unevenly paved streets.

Visitor Information

Tourist information for the whole country is handled by the **Croatian National Tourist Board** (Hrvatska Turistička Zajednica, or HTZ), which has a useful website offering detailed visitor information. The tourist board has information offices in several countries abroad. If you contact these before leaving, they will supply you with brochures covering the regions or activities you are most interested in. In addition, every town and city has an official tourist office, called a *turistički ured*, *turistička zajednica* or *turistički informativni centar*. These provide information on local sights, facilities and activities and, in many cases, will provide you with a free map. They will offer advice on local hotels and private accommodation, and on local agencies offering guided tours but cannot make bookings for you.

Also very useful is the network of county tourist boards with information on a particular region – for example, **Dubrovnik County Tourist Board** covers much of the Southern Dalmatian coast, as well as Korčula island. **Split County Tourist Board** covers the mainland coast around Split, as well as the islands of Šolta, Hvar, Vis and Brač.

Dubrovnik and **Split City Tourist offices** are usually open long hours, seven days a week, in the summer season. Hours vary during winter.

Trips and Tours

The old cities of Split and Dubrovnik are easy to explore on your own, but these labyrinthine places contain a wealth of history that is hard to discover unless you take one of the many guided walking tours offered by local agencies. Themed walking tours are a particularly good way of unearthing hidden detail; guided *Game of Thrones* walks by **Dubrovnik Walking Tours** and by **Split Walking Tour** will take you to shooting locations you might not find yourself.

Excursions offered by tourist agencies present a perfect way of roaming further afield. Popular trips from Dubrovnik include island cruises and trips to the Cetina Gorge, run by **Gulliver Travel**. From Split, both **Split Adventure** and **Go Adventure** organize activity trips to the Cetina Gorge and many other day trips.

The Biokovo mountain massif between Dubrovnik and Split is difficult to explore unless you take a jeep safari from **Biokovo Active Holidays** in Makarska.

The single most popular excursion destination on the Dalmatian islands is the Blue Cave on Biševo, reached by excursions offered by agencies such as **Alternatura** and the **Blue Cave Agency** in Komiža on Vis.

On Hvar, **Secret Hvar** and **Hvar Adventure** offer wine tasting, hiking, and tours of the historic hill villages in the middle of the island.

Based in Supetar, **Idi & Vidi** offers excellent cultural and gourmet tours of Brač.

Shopping

There's not much in the way of high-street shopping opportunities in Southern Dalmatia, but there are plenty of fascinating boutiques selling souvenirs and delicatessen goods tucked into the narrow alleys of central Dubrovnik and Split. Accessories and household goods produced by local designers come highly recommended and are on sale in many of the outlets listed in this guide (see p72).

The weekend designer market at the Prokurative in Split (see p33) showcases the work of many local creatives. The colourful open-air food markets at Gruž in Dubrovnik and just outside the walls of Diocletian's Palace in Split are the best places to browse for top-quality hams, cheeses, honeys and olive oils.

Dining

Adriatic seafood forms the backbone of the Dalmatian culinary repertoire, and you will find fresh fish, squid and shellfish dominating the menus of informal local eateries and fine-dining restaurants. Fresh white fish is at its best cooked simply – grilled or oven-baked with a pinch of salt and a generous splash of olive oil.

A whole new generation of restaurants in Dubrovnik, Split and Hvar town is beginning to mix local ingredients with global flavours, although restaurants in smaller centres tend to stick to the traditional offerings. Good risotto, pasta dishes and pizzas are available in most places, while Far Eastern cuisine enjoys a growing presence in Dubrovnik and Split. Splendid local wines are on offer pretty much everywhere, too, with red Plavac mali from Pelješac and dry white Pošip from Korčula among those demanding to be tasted.

Accommodation

The range and quality of hotels is rapidly improving with offerings in the boutique, spa and luxury-resort categories. Dubrovnik itself is particularly well served with four- and five-star options, many of which have wonderful views and bags of character.

Inexpensive tourist accommodation can also be had in the form of private rooms and apartments, many very comfortable indeed. Internet reservation sites such as **Booking.com** and services including **Airbnb.com** are the best places for such offerings.

Many of Southern Dalmatia's hostels come with a mixture of dorm beds and private doubles, and they are suitable for independent travellers of all ages.

The coastline is dotted with campsites, many boasting idyllic beach-side locations. Camping outside designated areas is prohibited in Croatia, so do not be tempted to stay overnight in woods or beaches that are not specifically reserved for campers.

Prices are at a premium in the summer season (roughly Jun to Sep), but excellent deals can be found outside of this period, especially for those who book online. Reservation sites offer some great deals, but also check the official website of the place you intend to stay at, as you may find a better price.

DIRECTORY

VISITOR INFORMATION

Croatian National Tourist Board
w croatia.hr

Dubrovnik City Tourist Office
MAP E8 ◾ Brsalje 5, Dubrovnik
020 312 011
w tzdubrovnik.hr

Dubrovnik County Tourist Board
MAP J8 ◾ Šipčine 2, 20 000 Dubrovnik
020 324 999
w visitdubrovnik.hr

Split City Tourist Office
MAP M2 ◾ Riva (Obala Hrvatskog narodnog preporoda) 9, Split
021 360 066
w visitsplit.com

Split County Tourist Board
MAP N6 ◾ Prilaz braće Kaliterna 10, 21 000 Split
021 490 032
w dalmatia.hr

TRIPS AND TOURS

Alternatura
MAP B5 ◾ Hrvatskih mučenika 2, Komiža, Vis
021 717 239
w alternatura.hr

Biokovo Active Holidays
MAP D4 ◾ Kralja Petra Krešimira IV 7b, Makarska
021 679 655
w biokovo.net

Blue Cave Agency
MAP B5 ◾ Trg kralja Tomislava 10, Komiža, Vis
021 713 752
w visbluecave.com

Dubrovnik Walking Tours
MAP J8 ◾ Ćira Carića 3
020 436 846
w dubrovnik-walking-tours.com

Gulliver Travel
MAP J8 ◾ Obala Stjepana Radića 25, Dubrovnik
020 410 888 w gulliver.hr

Hvar Adventure
MAP C4 ◾ Jurja Matijevića 20, Hvar town
021 717 813
w hvar-adventure.com

Idi & Vidi
MAP C3 ◾ Branka Deškovića 12, Supetar, Brač
091 159 7231
w idiividi.com

Secret Hvar
MAP C4 ◾ Dolac bb, Hvar town
021 717 615
w secrethvar.com

Split Adventure
MAP N6 ◾ Matije Gupca 26, Split 091 501 2913
w splitadventure.com

Go Adventure
MAP M3 ◾ Marulićeva 4
091 450 0400
w goadventurehr

Split Walking Tour
MAP N2 ◾ Dioklecijanova 3, Split 099 821 5383
w splitwalkingtour.com

ACCOMMODATION

Booking.com
w booking.com

Airbnb
w airbnb.com

Places to Stay

PRICE CATEGORIES
For a standard, double room per night (with breakfast if included), taxes and extra charges.

K under 900kn   **KK** 900–1,800kn   **KKK** over 1,800kn

Luxury Hotels

Sheraton Dubrovnik Riviera, Srebreno
MAP H6 ▪ Šetalište dr Franje Tuđmana 17 Srebreno ▪ 020 601 500 ▪ www.sheratondubrovnik riviera.com ▪ KK
This boldly contemporary boomerang-shaped building rises above the lovely Srebreno bay, 7 km (4 miles) southeast of Dubrovnik. As well as providing access to the beaches of the Dubrovnik Riviera, this hotel has indoor and outdoor pools, a state-of-the-art wellness centre, excellent restaurants and views of some gorgeous Adriatic sunsets.

Valamar Dubrovnik President
MAP H8 ▪ Iva Dulčića 142 ▪ 052 465 000 ▪ Closed Nov–Mar ▪ www.valamar. com ▪ KK
Located close to the Old Town and a few metres from the beach, this hotel is set on the scenic Babin kuk peninsula. All rooms have sea views and amenities include a wellness centre, indoor and outdoor pools and an award-winning restaurant.

Adriana, Hvar Town
MAP C4 ▪ Fabrika 28 ▪ 021 750 200 ▪ www. suncanihvar.com ▪ KKK
Situated right on Hvar harbour, this intimate hotel offers small but superbly equipped rooms decked out in lavender tones. The spa facilities are among the best on the island, and there is a small pool. The bar has great views of the harbour and is the ideal spot to relax over cocktails.

Excelsior, Dubrovnik
MAP H8 ▪ Frana Supila 12 ▪ 020 300 300 ▪ www. adriaticluxuryhotels.com ▪ KKK
With a seaside setting overlooking the Adriatic and the ancient Old Town, this is by far the finest hotel in Dubrovnik. The scenic views are combined with flawless service. It also boasts of an illustrious history of hosting royal guests and celebrities.

Grand Villa Argentina, Dubrovnik
MAP H8 ▪ Frana Supila 14 ▪ 020 300 300 ▪ www. adriaticluxuryhotels.com ▪ KKK
Restored to its full five-star glory, the Argentina (like its palatial sister villa, the Glavic) is in the district of Ploče, which is just to the east of the gate of the same name. The lovely sea-view rooms enjoy fabulous views of Old City.

Hilton Imperial Dubrovnik
MAP J8 ▪ Marijana Blažića 2 ▪ 020 320 320 ▪ www. dubrovnik.hilton.com ▪ KKK
Blending modern comfort and historic charisma, this hotel has 149 well-appointed guest rooms and suites, plus excellent leisure and dining options including the revamped Imperial Bar and Lounge, an indoor pool with sunroof and a fully equipped health club.

Lešić Dimitri Palace, Korčula Town
MAP E5 ▪ Don Pavla Pose 1–6 ▪ 020 715 560 ▪ Closed Nov–Mar ▪ www.ldpalace.com ▪ KKK
In a complex of medieval stone buildings, this boutique aparthotel's five residences have funky contemporary interiors. Facilities include private boats, a restaurant and a spa with Thai and Ayurveda therapists.

Park, Split
MAP N6 ▪ Hatzeov perivoj 3 ▪ 021 406 400 ▪ www. hotelpark-split.hr ▪ KKK
Regarded as one of the best hotels in Split, the Park is just set back from the waterfront at Bačvice. It boasts modern rooms, friendly staff and a good restaurant that has a palm-fringed terrace looking out to sea.

The Pucić Palace, Dubrovnik
MAP G9 ▪ Od Puča 1 ▪ 020 326 222 ▪ www.the pucicpalace.com ▪ KKK
Classical elegance and history pervade every aspect of this refurbished Renaissance palace. You can also be the envy of everyone in Dubrovnik by staying in the only luxury hotel within the Old City walls.

Villa Dubrovnik, Dubrovnik

MAP K9 ▪ Vlaha Bukovca 6 ▪ 020 500 300 ▪ www. villa-dubrovnik.hr ▪ KKK

Situated in a green oasis removed from the hustle and bustle of the Old City is this tranquil and luxurious retreat. All its comfortable rooms have balconies with views of the sea and Dubrovnik. The exclusive boat shuttle service into the Old Harbour adds that extra element of romance.

Resort Hotels

Hotel Odisej, Mljet National Park

MAP E6 ▪ Pomena ▪ 020 300 300 ▪ Closed Oct–Apr ▪ www. adriaticluxuryhotels.com ▪ K

This charming hotel within the verdant pine and oak tree forest is set in the heart of Mljet National Park. Rooms are fairly basic and a bit dated, though the apartment is more luxurious. The hotel has its own beach, plus a bar and a restaurant, but the real draw is the spectacular setting.

Amfora, Hvar Town

MAP C4 ▪ Ulica biskupa Jurja Dubokovića 5 ▪ 021 750 300 ▪ Closed Nov–Mar ▪ www. suncanihvar.com ▪ KK

The largest hotel in Hvar is staggering in its scale. Its plus points include welcoming staff, pleasant bedrooms, many with views of the Pakleni islands (see p34), and diverse sports facilities, including a large pool area that has cascading waterfalls and is surrounded by gardens.

Bluesun Elaphusa, Brač

MAP C4 ▪ Put Zlatnog rata 46, Bol ▪ 021 306 200 ▪ Closed Nov–Apr ▪ www. hotelelaphusa brac.com ▪ KK

Backed by pine woods and overlooking the sea, this big, modern four-star hotel has 300 rooms, six suites, a range of sports facilities and a wellness centre. It lies just a 5-minute walk from Bol's stunning Zlatni Rat beach.

Croatia, Cavtat

MAP H7 ▪ Frankopanska 10 ▪ 020 300 300 ▪ KK

Everything you would expect to find at a colossal five-star resort hotel is available at the Croatia: a fitness centre, sports facilities galore, a private beach, and indoor, outdoor and children's pools. Rooms are spacious and all have balconies (many with sea views).

Hotel Marko Polo, Korčula Town

MAP E5 ▪ Šetalište Frana Kršinića 102 ▪ 020 726 100 ▪ Closed Nov–Mar ▪ www.korcula-hotels. com ▪ KK

With great views across the harbour and Korčula's walled Old Town, this four-star hotel has an outdoor pool, a wellness centre and a small pebble beach. Most of the 103 rooms have sea views.

Issa, Vis Town

MAP B5 ▪ Šetalište Apolonija Zanelle 5 ▪ 021 711 164 ▪ www.hotelsvis. com ▪ KK

This unassuming three-star lacks many of the extras offered by other hotels but commands an idyllic location, with a pristine pebble beach immediately below. Boat-rental facilities and scuba-diving courses are available nearby, and most rooms come with views of Vis town's bay.

Kompas, Dubrovnik

MAP J8 ▪ Kardinala Stepinca 21 ▪ 020 300 300 ▪ www.adriaticluxury hotels.com ▪ KK

This four-star hotel is one of several supremely comfortable options overlooking the popular beach area of Lapad Bay. There's a modern spa centre offering beauty treatments, and the balconied rooms offfer stunning views.

Meteor, Makarska

MAP D4 ▪ Kralja Petra Krešimira IV 19 ▪ 021 564 200 ▪ www.hoteli-makarska.hr ▪ KK

The four-star Meteor is right beside Makarska's long pebble beach, its unique ziggurat shape ensuring that all of its balconied rooms offer guests a view. With spa facilities, large indoor and outdoor pools and a gym all under the same roof, this is also the ideal destination for a spot of holiday-time physical fine-tuning.

Radisson Blu Resort, Split

MAP C3 ▪ Put Trstenika 19 ▪ 021 303 030 ▪ www. radissonblu.com/resort-split ▪ KK

On the coast, 3 km (2 miles) east of Split's Old City, this hotel has smart, contemporary rooms and suites. There is also an outdoor pool, a pebble beach and a luxurious spa.

Velaris Resort, Supetar, Brač

MAP C3 ▪ Put Vele Luke 10 ▪ 021 606 606 ▪ www.velaris.hr ▪ KK

A group of three- and four-star hotels and villas occupying a wooded promontory west of Supetar, this is an ideal choice for a family holiday. It has many seaside activities, with a shingle beach on one side and a rockier area offering windsurfing, jet-skiing and scuba diving on the other.

Boutique Hotels

Bol, Bol, Brač

MAP C4 ▪ Hrvatskih domobrana 19 ▪ 021 635 660 ▪ www.hotel-bol.com ▪ KK

Situated close to the Zlatni Rat beach and few minutes from the sea and centre of Bol, this small hotel has a restaurant, bar, gym, sauna and outdoor pool. Some rooms have views of Vidova gora, the highest peak of the island of Brač.

Hotel Korsal, Korčula Town

MAP E5 ▪ Šetalište Frana Kršinića 80 ▪ 020 715 722 ▪ Closed Nov–Apr ▪ www. hotel-korsal.com ▪ KK

By the sea, just a 10-minute walk from the old town, this four-star family-run hotel has 19 rooms with wooden floors and a cheerful green-and-yellow colour scheme, plus a good restaurant with a waterside terrace.

Luxe, Split

MAP N3 ▪ Ul Kralja Zvonimira 6 ▪ 021 314 444 ▪ www.hotelluxesplit.com ▪ KK

This design hotel with its combination of bright purple fabrics and white surfaces and fittings, is brashly modern but not overpowering. Only a few steps from the Diocletian's Palace, the upper floors offer excellent views.

Marmont, Split

MAP L2▪ Zadarska 13 ▪ 021 308 060 ▪ www. marmonthotel.com ▪ KK

In a renovated 15th-century stone building in Split's historic centre, this four-star hotel has 21 rooms with smart decor and black marble bathrooms, plus a plush Presidential Suite.

Osam, Supetar, Brač

MAP C3 ▪ Vlačica 3 ▪ 021 552 333 ▪ www.hotel-osam.com ▪ KK

Perched above the seaside road that leads from Supetar harbour, this hotel offers smart and sleek rooms. Public areas are decorated in natural, minimalist colours. The restaurant offers an imaginative line in modern European-Dalmatian fusion, and the rooftop cocktail bar has outstanding views of the mainland. No children allowed.

Peristil, Split

MAP N2 ▪ Poljana kraljice Jelene 5 ▪ 021 329 070 ▪ www.hotelperistil.com ▪ KK

Set in the heart of Diocletian's Palace, the Peristil has 12 individually styled rooms at the heart of Diocletian's Palace. The decor is light and elegant, while friendly staff provide the finishing touch and impeccable service. The restaurant, Tiffany, serves exceptional Dalmatian cuisine. Book room 304, or the one overlooking the Peristyle (see p30).

Riva, Hvar Town

MAP C4 ▪ Riva 27 ▪ 021 750 100 ▪ Closed Nov–Mar ▪ www.suncani hvar.com ▪ KK

Right on Hvar harbour, just opposite the yacht berths, the Riva is one of the swankiest retreats on the island. Fully equipped rooms are decked out in warm colours with Pop Art details – try to secure a sea-facing room for the best views. With a wine bar and fusion-food restaurant also on site, the emphasis is on pure hedonism.

Villa Wolff, Dubrovnik

MAP J8 ▪ Nika i Meda Pučića 1 ▪ 020 438 710 ▪ www.villa-wolff.hr ▪ KK

This six-room boutique hotel offers pleasant rooms and attentive service. The waterfront restaurant, Casa, with its picturesque setting is perfect for dinner. Located just a few minutes drive from the Old City walls, the hotel has a wonderfully lush garden and promises great sea views.

Korčula de la Ville, Korčula Town

MAP E5 ▪ Obala dr Franje Tuđmana 5 ▪ 020 726 900 ▪ www.korcula-hotels.com ▪ KKK

This grand old hotel is a real period piece. It opened on the eve of World War I and has been refurbished in order to meld the splendours of the belle époque with modern facilities and furnishings. Right on the Old Town's waterfront and with a gorgeous palm-fringed cafe, it's the perfect pied à terre.

Prijeko Palace, Dubrovnik

MAP F8 ▪ Prijeko 22 ▪ 020 321 145 ▪ www.prijekopalace.com ▪ KKK

One of the Old City's more flamboyant former palaces provides a history-steeped home to this intimate hotel. Cosy, apartment-style rooms feature modern art on the walls and mini-kitchenettes in the corner. The restaurant serves outstanding food with a French-Dalmatian twist, and the cakes available in the downstairs café are superb.

Vestibul Palace, Split

MAP M2 ▪ Iza Vestibula 4 ▪ 021 329 329 ▪ www.vestibulpalace.com ▪ KKK

If you want to stay in the heart of Diocletian's Palace, then there are few choices better than the Vestibul, which is situated in a medieval stone palace that was built right on top of the emperor's former living quarters. The interior is something of a design masterpiece, mixing modern minimalism and straight lines with the exposed stonework of the original structure.

Small Hotels and B&Bs

Boutique Accommodation Mljet, Mljet

MAP E6 ▪ Goveđari 14 ▪ 020 744 140 ▪ www.boutiqueaccommodationmljet.com ▪ K

Some of the most romantic apartments in Dalmatia can be found in this restored school-house in the village of Goveđari, on the border of the Mljet National Park.

The decor strikes the perfect balance between modern conveniences and traditional furnishings, and there is a seemingly inexhaustible variety of idyllic local walks for the taking.

Ostrea, Mali Ston

MAP G6 ▪ Mali Ston ▪ 020 754 555 ▪ www.ostrea.hr ▪ K

Framed by the sea and the Pelješac hills, the Ostrea is an attractive small hotel within the former home of its proprietors, the Kralj family. Modern art adorns plain walls in the tasteful rooms and suite.

Villa Carrara, Trogir

MAP B3 ▪ Gradska 15 ▪ 021 881 075 ▪ www.karara-ap.com ▪ K

In Trogir's UNESCO-listed medieval Old City, this cosy B&B has eight rooms, all with antique furniture, wooden floors and some exposed beams and stonework. There's also a small breakfast room with elegant, wrought-iron chairs.

Villa Neretva, Metković

MAP F5 ▪ Krvavac II ▪ 020 672 200 ▪ www.hotel-villa-neretva.com ▪ K

Right at the heart of the Neretva Delta (see pp94–5), this waterfront restaurant with rooms provides comfortable accommodation. It is a good base for exploring this extraordinary waterscape, and it also runs boat tours for guests.

Villa Varoš, Split

MAP M5 ▪ Miljenka Smoje 1 ▪ 021 375 209 ▪ www.villavaros.hr ▪ K

A nicely restored medieval stone building offering neat double rooms and apartments this small family-run guesthouse is in the Varoš quarter, just 5 minutes' walk from Diocletian's Palace. The delightful neighbourhood is full of narrow alleys and small local restaurants. Breakfast is available from a nearby café, whereas lunch and dinner are also available in a nearby restaurant run by the same family.

Fresh* Sheets Kathedral, Dubrovnik

MAP G10 ▪ Bunićeva poljana 6 ▪ 091 896 7509 ▪ www.fresh-sheetskathedral.com ▪ KK

Housed in a historic church-owned building behind the cathedral, Fresh* Sheets has an unique location. It offers double rooms, family suites and apartments equipped with modern fittings. Wake up in the heart of Dubrovnik before the tour groups arrive and enjoy a delicious breakfast in the square below.

Hotel Villa Pattiera, Cavtat

MAP H7 ▪ Trumbićev put 9 ▪ 020 478 800 ▪ Closed Nov–Mar ▪ www.villa-pattiera.hr ▪ KK

This renovated historic villa is the birthplace of the Croatian opera star Tino Pattiera. Now a family-run boutique hotel overlooking Cavtat's harbour, it has 12 stylish and individually decorated rooms. All have either a balcony or a private terrace. The hotel's excellent restaurant, Dalmacija, serves traditional cuisine and has outdoor tables.

For a key to hotel price categories see p112

**San Giorgio,
Vis Town**

MAP B5 ▪ Petra
Hektorovića 2 ▪ 021 607
630 ▪ www.hotelsan
giorgiovis.com ▪ Closed
Nov–Mar ▪ KK

The Kut area of Vis town
is the location for this
small, family-owned
hotel. The historic setting,
large guest rooms, tranquil
location and excellent
seafood restaurant all
ensure a very pleasant
stay. Some rooms have
views to the sea.

**Boutique Hotel Stari
Grad, Dubrovnik**

MAP F8 ▪ Od Sigurate 4
▪ 020 322 244 ▪ www.
hotelstarigrad.com
▪ KKK

The more affordable
of the two hotels in
the Old City, this intimate,
eight-room establish-
ment is tucked away in
a narrow street just
off Stradun, the main
thoroughfare. It offers
the highest level of
contemporary luxury.
The rooftop restaurant
provides prime views
of the Old Town and
Adriatic Sea.

Budget

**Biličić Guesthouse,
Dubrovnik**

Off MAP ▪ Priževna 2
▪ 020 417 152 ▪ K

Cosy en-suite rooms
and a lovely walled garden
mark this out as one of
the prettiest guesthouses
in Dubrovnik. It's situated
just up the hill from
Dubrovnik's walls, and
the stroll down into the
Old City is a great way
to start the day. This is
a popular place to stay,
so be sure to book in
advance.

**City Walls Hostel,
Dubrovnik**

MAP F10 ▪ Svetog Šimuna
15 ▪ 091 416 1919 ▪ www.
citywallshostel.com
▪ Closed Dec–Feb ▪ K

Based in an old stone
building near Dubrovnik's
seaward walls, this
place is popular with
backpackers. It offers
dormitory rooms, compli-
mentary breakfast, a
communal kitchen and
free internet access to all.

Goli + Bosi, Split

MAP L2 ▪ Morpurgova
Poljana 2 ▪ 021 510 999
▪ www.gollybossy.com ▪ K

In a former department
store in Split's Old City,
this slick hostel has
28 rooms from eight-bed
dorms to doubles, all with
en-suite, air conditioning
and free Wi-Fi. There's
also a restaurant-bar.

**Green Lizard,
Hvar Town**

MAP C4 ▪ Domovinskog
rata 13 ▪ 021 742 560
▪ www.greenlizard.hr
▪ Closed Nov–Apr ▪ K

Set above Hvar's Old
Town, a 10-minute walk
uphill from the harbour
and with gorgeous views,
is this welcoming hostel.
There are several shared
rooms with mobile air
conditioning unit, having
bunk beds, two doubles
with en-suites, free Wi-Fi
and a communal outdoor
kitchen and barbecue
area in the pretty garden.

**Hostel Makarska,
Makarska**

MAP D4 ▪ Prvosvibanjska
15 ▪ 091 256 7212
▪ www.hostelmakarska.
com ▪ K

Located on one of central
Makarska's narrow
streets, this converted

family house offers a
mixture of dormitory
beds, private double
rooms and family-sized
self-catering apartments.
Its location in a palm-
shaded garden provides
an extra touch of magic.

**Marinero Hostel,
Hvar Town**

MAP C4 ▪ Put svetog
Marka 7 ▪ 091 410 2751
▪ www.hostel-marinero-
hr.book.direct ▪ K

This tall and narrow stone
house just around the
corner from the harbour
features airy dorm rooms
with bunk beds. The
ground floor is occupied
by the Marinero restau-
rant, with rows of outdoor
benches that are great
for big groups. With
neighbouring alleys
packed with bars and
food outlets, it's the kind
of location that suits late-
to-bed types.

**Old Town Hostel,
Dubrovnik**

MAP F8 ▪ Od Sigurate 7
▪ 020 322 007 ▪ www.
dubrovnikoldtown
hostel.com ▪ Closed
Dec–Feb ▪ K

This hostel in a pretty
Baroque stone building
has 24 beds within four
dorms and three doubles
. All rooms are white-
washed, with wooden
floors and old-fashioned
bunk beds. There's also a
kitchen and a common
room with a TV. There's
no air con, however.

**Vila Micika,
Dubrovnik**

MAP J8 ▪ Mata Vodopića
10 ▪ 098 243 717 ▪ www.
vilamicika.hr ▪ K

Simple accommodation is
on offer here in a typical
Dalmatian stone villa

in Lapad. There are just eight bedrooms, so book well in advance. All rooms are equipped with air conditioning and free Wi-Fi, and the villa also has a car park, a barbecue and a communal terrace.

Campsites

Antony Boy, Viganj
MAP E5 ▪ Viganj ▪ 020 719 077 ▪ www.antony-boy.com ▪ K

A level site partly shaded by olive trees, Antony Boy is right next to Viganj's pebbly Punta beach, something of a mecca for European windsurfers. The site itself comes with windsurf hire and a windsurf school and it also hires bikes to those who want to explore the semi-abandoned villages just inland.

Camping Grebišće, Jelsa
MAP C4 ▪ Grebišće ▪ 021 761 191 ▪ www.grebisce. hr ▪ Closed Nov–Apr ▪ K

Few campsites are better placed for an untroubled beach holiday than Hvar's Grebišće, which occupies a grassy bluff directly above Grebišće beach, a famously shallow bay that is sandy underfoot and perfect for kids. The centre of Jelsa is about 1.5 km (1 mile) to the west – ideal for a walk or a pleasant drive or cycle.

Camping Port 9, Korčula Town
MAP E5 ▪ Dubrovačka cesta 19 ▪ 020 726 801 ▪ Closed Oct–May ▪ www. korcula-hotels.com ▪ K

Just 2 km (1 mile) from the historic centre of Korčula town and 50 m (165 ft) from a beach, this

campsite has 124 pitches. The facilities include a shop and a restaurant. There is a small extra charge for parking. Under-12s pay a reduced rate.

Camping Solitudo, Dubrovnik
MAP J8 ▪ Vatroslava Lisinskog 60 ▪ 020 448 686 ▪ Closed Nov–Mar ▪ www.camping-adriatic. com ▪ K

The closest campsite to Dubrovnik's Old City is just a 10-minute bus ride away. It has 393 pitches, a modest restaurant and an outdoor swimming pool. Surrounded by pine trees, it is 200 m (655 ft) from the shore. There are reduced rates for under-10s, making this a popular family option.

Camping Stobreč, Split
MAP C3 ▪ Sv Lovre 6 ▪ Stobreč, Split ▪ 021 325 426 ▪ www.campingsplit. com ▪ K

This well-equipped site at the eastern edge of town, 6 km (4 miles) from the centre, is perfectly placed beside the main road towards the Makarska Riviera. It has its own stretch of seafront and is also well positioned for the long pebble beach at Žnjan, one of Split's most popular family destinations.

Camping Trsteno, Trsteno
MAP G6 ▪ Trsteno ▪ 020 751 060 ▪ Closed mid-Oct–Mar ▪ www.trsteno. hr ▪ K

Located up the hill from the Trsteno Arboretum, this pleasant, small-scale campsite is situated amid

olive groves. Stairs lead to a pebble beach. On-site facilities include a shop and a restaurant.

Camp Jure, Makarska
MAP D4 ▪ Ivana Gorana Kovačića bb ▪ 021 616 063 ▪ www.kamp-jure. com ▪ K

At the western end of town, superbly placed for Makarska's long pebbly beach, is this large site shaded by tamarisks. It's a good spot for paragliding and parasailing and other beach sports, and the centre of Makarska is only 20 minutes away on foot.

Camp Meteor, Bol
MAP C4 ▪ Hrvatskih domobrana 1 ▪ 021 635 630 ▪ K

One of several camps sheltering in the olive groves on the north side of town, Meteor is a friendly family-run place. It's far enough away from the seafront to be relaxing but is still a good base for the daytime bustle of Zlatni Rat beach.

Camp Vira, Hvar Town
MAP C4 ▪ Vira ▪ 021 741 803 ▪ www.campvira.com ▪ Closed Oct–Apr ▪ K

Occupying its own bay 4 km (2 miles) from Hvar town, Vira runs behind a beautiful pebble beach, with pitches for caravans and tents set out on a terraced, pine-shaded slope. Kayaks can be hired on the beach, activities are organized for kids, and there is a bar-restaurant on site.

For a key to hotel price categories see p112

General Index

Acknowledgments

Author

Based in Scotland, Robin and Jenny McKelvie are a formidable husband-and-wife travel-writing team. Between them they have visited more than 70 countries, and have co-authored guides to Croatia, Latvia, Slovenia and Dubai.

Thanks to the Croatian National Tourist Board, especially Andrea Petrov and Renata Dezeljin in Zagreb, and Josip Lozić in London. Thanks also to Zrinka Marinović and Nikolina Vicelić at Adriatic Luxury Hotels in Dubrovnik.

Additional Contributor

Jonathan Bousfield has been travelling in Central & Eastern Europe for many years. He has authored a number of DK Eyewitness guides and Rough Guides titles.

Publishing Director Georgina Dee

Publisher Vivien Antwi

Design Director Phil Ormerod

Editorial Sophie Adam, Michelle Crane, Rachel Fox, Cincy Jose, Alison McGill, Sally Schafer, Sands Publishing Solutions

Cover Design Bess Daly, Maxine Pedliham

Design Tessa Bindloss, Richard Czapnik, Bhavika Mathur, Marisa Renzullo

Picture Research Susie Peachey, Ellen Root, Lucy Sienkowska, Oran Tarjan

Cartography Suresh Kumar, Casper Morris, Reetu Pandey

DTP Jason Little

Production Luca Bazzoli

Factchecker Natasa Novakovic

Proofreader Clare Peel

Indexer Hilary Bird

Illustrator Chapel Design & Marketing

First edition created by DP Services, a division of Duncan Petersen Publishing Ltd

Revisions Hansa Babra, Parnika Bagla, Sumita Khatwani, Shikha Kulkarni, Natasa Novakovic, Manjari Thakur, Tanveer Zaidi

Commissioned Photography Lucio Rossi, Tony Souter

Picture Credits

123RF.com: Andrey Bodrov 71b.

Alamy Stock Photo: The Art Archive / Gianni Dagli Orti 33bl; Dario Bajurin 1; Ivan Batinic 22br; Stephen Coyne 94tl; Richard Cummins 92br; DustyDingo 54t; Alexei Fateev 95tr; funkyfood London - Paul Williams 6cr, 24–5; Ian Furniss 62bl; hemis.fr / Rene Mattes 47tr; imageBROKER / Günter Flegar 2tr, 38–9, / Günter Lenz 47cl; Ingolf Pompe 41 4t; Bjanka Kadic 46tl, 96c; Justin Kase zsixz 60tr; KEYSTONE Pictures USA 41tl; LatitudeStock 98cla; Nino Marcutti 52br, 91cr; Itsik Marom 58tr; Odyssey-Images 51cl; Panama 40bc; photisca 51tr; Pixel 8 21tl; Dave Porter 21bl; Bart Pro 52tl; Michael Robertson 55tr; traveler 4cr; Travelfile 4b, 35bl; V&A Images 40cr; Scott Wilson 8–9; ZUMA Press, Inc. 63cl; Piotr Zadroga 61tr.

AWL Images: Sabine Lubenow 53cl.

Restoran Baletna Škola: 93cr.

Bota Šare: 75cr.

Bugenvila Cavtat: 56tl.

Club Lazareti: Fjaka 73cr.

Corbis: Bettmann 33cl.

Croatian National Tourist Board: Ivo Biocina 18cla; Aleksandar Gospić 23crb; Studio Gobbo 32bl.

D'Vino Wine Bar: 74tl.

Dorling Kindersley: Courtesy of the Galerija Meštrović, Muzeji Ivana Meštrovića / Lucio Rossi 46cb.

Dreamstime.com: Ailenn 68c; Mila Atkovska 15crb; Baloncici 10cl; Artur Bogacki 69tl; Olena Buyskykh 10cla; Ccat82 4cl; Mario Čehulić 86tl; Marilyn Ching 96b; Daniel M. Cisilino 11crb, 12c, 14cla, 14–15, 67tr; Sorin Colac 2tl, 8–9; Andras Csontos 7tl; Dbajurin 78bl; Dreamer4787 66cr; Donyanedomam 11bl; Stefano Ember 11cra; Luisa Vallon Fumi 28cla; Artur Gabrysiak 14bl; Janos Gaspar 68b, 89cl; Inavanhateren 66cla, 76tl, 81cr; Ivansmuk 59cl; Jarnogz 30bl; Jasmina 12–13, 13b, 36–7, 49tl, 50br; Joymsk 29bl; Kemaltaner 30br; Aleksandrs Kosarevs 12bl; Kviktor 26br; Landd09 54br, 60b; Lianem 90tl, 94cr; Lukaszimilena 7br, 11br, 36br; Marcinknop 95br; Mareticd 78tr, 81tl; Marinv 55cl; Galina Mikhalishina 4crb; Evgeniya Moroz 34bl; Mrakhr 22clb; Mtr 20–21; Nadtochiy 31tl; Nevenm 57tr; Nightman1965 12cla; Phant 10crb, 26–7; Saša Prijić 43cr; Reddogs 15ca; Rndmst 26cl, 36cl, 44tl; Salajean 28bl; Sjankauskas 3tr, 102–3; Nikolai Sorokin 11c, 61cl, 90br; Kiril Stanchev 88b; Paula Stanley 45tc; Serghei Starus 84–5; Aleksandar Todorovic 27crb; Tuomaslehtinen 10bl, 20clb, 48cl; Vesnyanka 87br; Birute Vijeikiene 30-1c; Xbrchx 3tl, 11tl, 22–3, 28–9, 31cr, 32t, 34–5, 42tl, 42b, 49b, 64–5, 77t, 79cl, 80b, 87tr.

Gaixa Hvar: Damir Fabijanic 83cl.

Getty Images: AFP PHOTO / Andrej Isakovic 53tr; OGphoto 18–19.

Hula Hula Hvar Town: Marko Delbello Ocepek 82tl.

Irish Pub "The Gaffe": 74br.

Konobia Adio Mare: 57cl.

Korta Katarina Winery: 100t.

Mediterranean Film Festival: 62tr.

Medusa: Tinka 72bl.

Restaurant Nautika: 56br

Paradox Wine & Cheese Bar: 92tl

Rex by Shutterstock: imageBROKER / Günter Flegar 50t; SIPA / CROPIX / Zvonimir Barisin 63tr; SIPA PRESS 41clb, 41br.

Robert Harding Picture Library: Gonzalo Azumendi 70tl; Gunter Flegar 97cl; LOOK Bildagentur der Fotografen / Konrad Wothe 87br; Martin Moxter 18bl; Bernd Rohrschneider 45bl; Martin Siepmann 4clb; Matthew Williams-Ellis 4cla, 34crb.

Studio Magenta: Bakus Restaurant 101cr.

SuperStock: Mauritius / Wolfgang Weinhäupl 58bl; Prisma / Album 17br.

Trpanj Tourist Board: 99b

Uje: 59tr.

Cover

Front and spine: **Getty Images:** Matthew Williams-Ellis / robertharding

Back: **AWL Images:** Doug Pearson tr **Dreamstime.com:** Oriontrail cla, Rudi1976 crb, Xbrchx tl. **Getty Images:** Matthew Williams-Ellis / robertharding bc

Pull Out Map Cover

Getty Images: Matthew Williams-Ellis / robertharding

All other images © Dorling Kindersley
For further information see: www.dkimages.com

As a guide to abbreviations in visitor information blocks: **Adm** = admission charge.

FSC
www.fsc.org
MIX
Paper from responsible sources
FSC™ C018179

DK | Penguin Random House

Printed and bound in China

First Edition 2006

Published in Great Britain by Dorling Kindersley Limited 80 Strand, London WC2R 0RL

Published in the United States by DK Publishing, 345 Hudson Street, New York, New York 10014

Copyright © 2006, 2019 Dorling Kindersley Limited

A Penguin Random House Company

18 19 20 21 10 9 8 7 6 5 4 3 2 1

**Reprinted with revisions
2008, 2010, 2012, 2014, 2017, 2019**

A CIP catalogue record is available from the British Library.

A catalogue record for this book is available from the Library of Congress

ISSN 1479 344X
ISBN 978-0-2413-6179-5

SPECIAL EDITIONS OF DK TRAVEL GUIDES

DK Travel Guides can be purchased in bulk quantities at discounted prices for use in promotions or as premiums. We also offer special editions and personalized jackets, corporate imprints, and excerpts from all our books, tailored to meet your needs.

To find out more, please contact:

in the US
specialsales@dk.com
in the UK
travelguides@uk.dk.com
in Canada
specialmarkets@dk.com
in Australia
**penguincorporatesales@
penguinrandomhouse.com.au**

Phrase Book

Pronounciation Guide

c – "ts" as in rats	*č* – "ch" as in church
ć – "t" is a soft t	*đ* – "d" as in endure
g – "g" as in get	*j* – "y" as in yes
š – "sh" as in shoe	*ž* – "J" as in Jacques
aj – "igh" as in night	

In an Emergency

Help!	Pomoć!	*pomoch!*
Stop!	Stani!	*stahnee!*
Call a doctor!	Zovite doktora!	*zoveetey doktorah!*
Call an ambulance!	Zovite hitnu pomoć!	*zoveetey heetnoo pomoch!*
Call the police!	Zovite policiju!	*zoveetey poleetseeyoo!*
Call the fire brigade!	Zovite vatrogasce!	*zoveetey vatrohgastsay!*

Communication Essentials

Yes	Da	*dah*
No	Ne	*ney*
Please	Polim vas	*moleem vas*
Thank you	Hvala	*hvahlah*
Excuse me	Oprostite	*oprosteetey*
Hello	Dobar dan	*dobar dan*
Goodbye	Doviđenja	*doveedjenya*
Good night	Laku noć	*lakoo noch*
Yesterday	Jučer	*yoocher*
Today	Danas	*danas*
Tomorrow	Sutra	*sootrah*
Here	Tu	*too*
There	Tamo	*tahmoh*
What?	Što?	*shtoh*
When?	Kada?	*kada*
Why?	Zašto?	*zashtoh*
Where?	Gdje?	*gdyey*

Useful Phrases

How are you?	Kako ste?	*kakoh stey*
Very well, thank you	Dobro, hvala	*dobroh, hvahlah*
Where is/are...?	Gdje je/su?	*gdyey yey/soo?*
How can I get to...?	Kako mogu doći do...?	*kakoh mogoo dochee doh...*
Do you speak English?	Govorite li engleski?	*govoreetey lee engleskee?*
I don't understand	Ne razumijem	*nay razoomeeyem*
Could you speak more slowly please?	Molim vas, možete li govoriti sporije?	*moleem vas, mozhetey lee govoreetee sporiyey?*
I'm sorry	Žao mi je	*zhaoh mee yey*

Useful Words

big	veliko	*veleekoh*
small	malo	*mahloh*
hot	vruć	*vrooch*
cold	hladan	*hlahdan*
good	dobar	*dobar*
bad	loš	*losh*
open	otvoreno	*otvohrenoh*
closed	zatvoreno	*zatvohrenoh*
left	lijevo	*leeyevoh*
right	desno	*desnoh*
straight on	ravno	*ravnoh*
near	blizu	*bleezoo*
far	daleko	*dalekoh*
up	gore	*gorey*
down	dolje	*dolyey*
early	rano	*ranoh*
late	kasno	*kasnoh*
entrance	ulaz	*oolaz*
exit	izlaz	*eezlaz*
toilet	WC	*Vey tsey*
more	više	*veeshey*
less	manje	*manyey*

Shopping

How much does this cost?	Koliko ovo košta?	*kolikoh ovoh koshta?*
I would like...	Volio bih...	*volioh bee...*
Do you have...?	Imate li...?	*eematey lee...?*
I'm just looking	Samo gledam	*Samoh gledam*
Do you take credit cards?	Primate li kreditne kartice?	*preematey lee credeetney carteetsey?*
What time do you open/close?	Kad otvarate/ zatvarate?	*kad otvaratey/ zatvaratey?*
This one	Ovaj	*ov-igh*
That one	Onaj	*on-igh*
expensive	skupo	*skoopoh*
cheap	jeftino	*yefteenoh*
size (clothes)	veličina	*veleechinah*
size (shoes)	broj	*broy*
white	bijelo	*beeyeloh*
black	crno	*tsrnoh*
red	crveno	*tsrvenoh*
yellow	žuto	*zhootoh*
green	zeleno	*zelenoh*
blue	plavo	*plavoh*
bakery	pekara	*pekarah*
bank	banka	*bankah*
book shop	knjižara	*knyeezharah*
butcher's	mesnica	*mesnitsah*
cake shop	slastičarna	*slasteecharnah*
chemist's	apoteka	*apohtekah*
fishmonger's	ribarnica	*reebarnitsah*
market	tržnica	*trzhneetsah*
hairdresser's	frizer	*freezer*
newsagent's	trafika	*trafeekah*
post office	pošta	*poshtah*

Sightseeing

art gallery	galerija umjetnina	*galereeyah oomyetneenah*
cathedral	katedrala	*katedralah*
church	crkva	*tsrkvah*
library	knjižnica	*knyeezhneetsah*
museum	muzej	*moozey*
tourist information centre	turistički ured	*tooreesteechkey oored*
bus station	autobusni kolodvor	*aootoboosnee kolodvor*
railway station	željeznički kolodvor	*zhelyeznickih kolodvor*

Staying in a Hotel

Do you have a vacant room?	Imate li sobu?	*eematey lee soboo*
double room	dvokrevetna soba	*dvokrevetnah sobah*
single room	jednokrevetna soba	*yednokrevetnah sobah*
room with a bath	soba sa kupaonicom	*sobah sah koopaoneetsom*
shower	tuš	*toosh*
I have a reservation	Imam rezervaciju	*eemam rezervatseeyoo*

Eating Out

Have you got	Imate li	eematey lee
a table for...?	stol za...?	stol zah
I want to	Želim	Zheleem
reserve a table	rezervirati stol	rezerveeratee stol
The bill please	Molim vas,	moleem vas,
	račun	rachoon
I am	Ja sam	yah sam
a vegetarian	vegetarijanac	vegetareeyanats
waiter/waitress	konobar/	konobar/
	konobarica	konobaritsah
menu	jelovnik	yelovneek
wine list	vinska karta	veenskah kartah
glass	čaša	chashah
bottle	boca	botsah
knife	nož	nozh
fork	vilica	veeleetsa
spoon	žlica	zhleetsah
breakfast	doručak	doroochak
lunch	ručak	roochak
dinner	večera	vecherah
main course	glavno jelo	glavnoh yeloh
starters	predjela	predyelah

Menu Decoder

bijela riba	beeyelah reebah	"white" fish
blitva	bleetvah	Swiss chard
brudet	broodet	fish stew
ćevapčići	chevapcheechee	meatballs
crni rižot	tsrnee reezhot	black risotto
desert	desert	dessert
glavno jelo	glavnoh yeloh	main course
grah	grah	beans
gulaš	goolash	goulash
jastog	yastog	lobster
juha	yoohah	soup
kuhano	koohanoh	cooked
maslinovo	masleenovoh	olive oil
ulje	oolyey	
meso na	mesoh nah	barbecued meat
žaru	zharoo	
miješano	meejeshanoh	mixed grilled
meso	mesoh	meats
na žaru	nah zharoo	barbecued
ocat	otsat	vinegar
palačinke	palacheenkay	pancakes
papar	papar	pepper
pečeno	pechenoh	baked
piletina	peeleteenah	chicken
plava riba	plavah reebah	"blue" fish
predjelo	predyeloh	starters
prilog	preelog	side dish
pršut	prshoot	smoked ham
pržene	przhene	fried squid
lignje	leegnyey	
prženo	przhenoh	fried
ramsteak	ramsteyk	rump steak
ražnjići	razhnyeechee	pork kebabs
riba na	reebah nah	barbecued fish
žaru	zharoo	
rižot frutti	reezhot frootee	seafood risotto
di mare	dee marey	
rižot sa	reezhot sah	scampi risotto
škampima	shkampeemah	
salata	salatah	salad
salata od	salatah od	octopus salad
hobotnice	hobotneetsey	
sarma	sarmah	cabbage leaves
sir	seer	cheese
sladoled	sladoled	ice cream
slana srdela	slanah srdelah	salted sardines
škampi na	shkampee nah	scampi in tomato
buzaru	boozaroo	and onion sauce
školjke na	shkolkay nah	shellfish in
buzaru	boozaroo	tomato sauce
špageti frutti	shpagetee frootee	spaghetti with
di mare	dee marey	seafood
sol	sol	salt
tjestenina	tjesteneenah	pasta
ulje	oolyey	oil

Drinks

bijelo vino	beeyeloh veenoh	white wine
crno vino	tsrnoh veenoh	red wine
gazirana/	gazeeranah/	sparkling/still
negazirana	neygazeeranah	mineral water
mineralna	meeneralnah	
voda	vodah	
čaj	ch-igh	tea
kava	kavah	coffee
pivo	peevoh	beer

Numbers

0	nula	noolah
1	jedan	yedan
2	dva	dvah
3	tri	tree
4	četiri	cheteeree
5	pet	pet
6	šest	shest
7	sedam	sedam
8	osam	osam
9	devet	devet
10	deset	deset
11	jedanaest	yedanighst
12	dvanaest	dvahnighst
13	trinaest	treenighst
14	četrnaest	chetrnighst
15	petnaest	petnighst
16	šesnaest	shestnighst
17	sedamnaest	sedamnighst
18	osamnaest	osamnighst
19	devetnaest	devetnighst
20	dvadeset	dvahdeset
21	dvadeset i	dvahdeset ee
	jedan	yedan
30	trideset	treedeset
31	trideset i	treedeset ee
	jedan	yedan
40	četrdeset	chetrdeset
50	pedeset	pedeset
60	šezdeset	shezdeset
70	sedamdeset	sedamdeset
80	osamdeset	osamdeset
90	devedeset	devedeset
100	sto	stoh
101	sto i jedan	stoh ee yedan
102	sto i dva	stoh ee dvah
200	dvjesto	dvyestoh
500	petsto	petstoh
700	sedamsto	sedamstoh
900	devetsto	devetstoh
1,000	tisuću	teesoochoo

Time

One minute	jedna	yednah
	minuta	meenootah
One hour	jedan sat	yedan saht
Half an hour	pola sata	polah sahtah
Monday	ponedjeljak	ponedyelyak
Tuesday	utorak	ootorak
Wednesday	srijeda	sreejedah
Thursday	četvrtak	chetvrtak
Friday	petak	petak
Saturday	subota	soobotah
Sunday	nedjelja	nedyelyah

Central and Southern Dalmatia Index

Dubrovnik Old Town Index